RENEW INTERNATIONAL

WHY CATHOLIC?
JOURNEY THROUGH THE CATECHISM

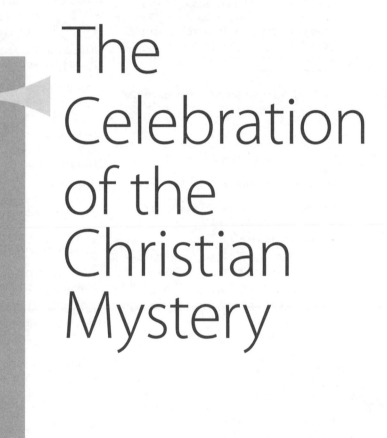

The Celebration of the Christian Mystery

RENEW
INTERNATIONAL

The publisher gratefully acknowledges use of the following:

Scripture quotations from the *New Revised Standard Version Bible* (containing the Old and New Testaments with the Apocryphal/Deuterocanonical Books), © 1989 by the Division of Christian Education of the National Council of the Churches of Christ in the U.S.A., and are used with permission. All rights reserved.

English translation of the *Catechism of the Catholic Church for the United States of America* © 1994, United States Conference of Catholic Bishops–Libreria Editrice Vaticana. English translation of the *Catechism of the Catholic Church:* Modifications from the *Editio Typica* © 1997, United States Conference of Catholic Bishops–Libreria Editrice Vaticana. Used with permission.

The United States Catholic Catechism for Adults © 2006 United States Conference of Catholic Bishops. Used with permission.

For online access to an interactive site allowing users to search the full text of the *Catechism of the Catholic Church,* go to:
www.vatican.va/archive/ENG0015/_INDEX.HTM

The following documents are all © United States Conference of Catholic Bishops:

Prayer for Marriage

Jubilee 2000; A Year of the Lord's Favor: A Reflection on Forgiveness and Reconciliation © 2001

Built of Living Stones © 2001

Celebrating the Sacrament of Penance Questions and Answers © 2003

Popular Devotional Practices: Basic Questions and Answers © 2003

All USCCB documents used with permission.

Excerpts from the English translation of Eucharistic Prayer IV (adapted) from the *Roman Missal* © 2010, International Committee on English in the Liturgy, Inc. (ICEL); excerpt from the English translation of *Rite of Christian Initiation of Adults* © 1985, ICEL; excerpts from the English translation of *Pastoral Care of the Sick: Rites of Anointing and Viaticum* (adapted) © 1982, ICEL; excerpt from the English translation of *Ordination of Deacons, Priests, and Bishops* © 1975, ICEL. All rights reserved.

Excerpt adapted from *Gift of Peace: Personal Reflections by Joseph Cardinal Bernardin* © 1997 Archdiocese of Chicago. Used with permission

Excerpt from *Prayers for the Domestic Church* by Edward Hayes © 2007 Ave Maria Press. All rights reserved.

"Blessed are You, Lord" prayer from *Prayers for the Domestic Church* by Edward Hayes © 2007 Ave Maria Press. Used with permission.

Excerpt adapted from *Living Eucharist: Gathered, Nourished, Sent* (supplement) by Bishop Robert Lynch. © 2010 Diocese of St. Petersburg. Used with permission.

"Built of Living Stones" prayer written by Fr. Edward Hislop © Diocese of Helena. Used with permission.

All of the quotes from papal and conciliar documents used in this book are from the English translation as presented by the Vatican website.

NIHIL OBSTAT
Monsignor James M. Cafone, S.T.D.
Censor Librorum

IMPRIMATUR
Most Reverend John J. Myers, J.C.D., D.D.
Archbishop of Newark

Cover design by James F. Brisson;
Book design and layout by Kathrine Forster Kuo

© 2002, 2005, 2006, 2007, 2010
by RENEW International

ISBN 978-1-935532-02-6
(2005-6 editions ISBN 1-930978-36-7;
2002 edition ISBN 1-930978-15-4)

RENEW International
1232 George Street
Plainfield, NJ 07062-1717
Phone: 908-769-5400
Fax: 908-769-5660
www.renewintl.org
www.WhyCatholic.org

Printed and bound in the United States of America.

Contents

Acknowledgments

RENEW International gratefully acknowledges those who have contributed to this work:

Piloters

Small Christian community members who piloted the materials and offered helpful insights.

Music References

All of the songs suggested in this book are available on a CD produced by RENEW International. See more details on page 97; full details at **www.renewintl.org/store**

The publishers of copyright songs suggested in this book are:

GIA
GIA Publications, Inc.
7404 South Mason Avenue
Chicago, IL 60638
Phone 800-442-1358 or 708-496-3800
Fax 708-496-3828
Website www.giamusic.com
E-mail custserv@giamusic.com

White Dove
White Dove Productions, Inc.
Phone 520-219-3824
Website
www.whitedoveproductions.com
E-mail
    info@whitedoveproductions.com

OCP
Oregon Catholic Press Publications
5536 NE Hassalo
Portland, OR 97213
Phone 800-LITURGY (548-8749)
Fax 800-4-OCP-FAX (462-7329)
Website www.ocp.org
E-mail liturgy@ocp.org

Foreword

My calling as a bishop challenges me to ever seek means to assist solid faith formation and growth in holiness. Foundational in meeting this need is the *Catechism of the Catholic Church*, which so magnificently conveys the wisdom of the Holy Spirit in guiding the Church's tradition in following Jesus Christ.

The Introduction to the U.S. bishops' document *Our Hearts Were Burning Within Us* speaks of how disciples of Jesus share in proclaiming the Good News to the entire world.

Every disciple of the Lord Jesus shares in this mission. To do their part, adult Catholics must be mature in faith and well equipped to share the Gospel, promoting it in every family circle, in every church gathering, in every place of work, and in every public forum. They must be women and men of prayer whose faith is alive and vital, grounded in a deep commitment to the person and message of Jesus.

Why Catholic? Journey through the Catechism is well designed to enable this goal to become reality. It faithfully breaks open the contents of the *Catechism* for reflection and assimilation by individuals or participants in small faith-sharing groups. The sharing enables participants to take greater personal ownership of their faith and to move from an inherited faith to deep faith conviction.

This exploration of divinely revealed truth has a formative effect on peoples' lives. The "yes" of consent to faith emulates Mary's fiat, her "yes" to God's will. A prayerful openness to God's will is the path to holiness.

Why Catholic? seeks to be an instrument for faith formation and a call to holiness. Saints in everyday life are the strength of the Church, which is always renewing itself in fidelity to the mission of Christ and in service to the needs of our society. I heartily commend this effort in making the *Catechism of the Catholic Church* more accessible to the faithful.

Most Reverend John J. Myers, J.C.D., D.D.
Archbishop of Newark

Presenting RENEW International

Why Catholic? Journey through the Catechism is a four-year process of evangelization and adult faith formation developed by RENEW International.

The RENEW process, both parish-based and diocesan-wide, was first developed and implemented in the Archdiocese of Newark, New Jersey. Its success there led other dioceses, in the United States, and in other countries, to bring RENEW to their people and parish communities. In the three decades since its vibrant beginnings, RENEW International has touched the lives of 25 million people in over 150 dioceses in the United States and 23 countries throughout the world. RENEW International has grown organically from its original single RENEW process. Materials and training have been offered in over 40 languages–not just translated but adapted to specific cultures. We have added specific pastoral outreach to campuses, and to young adults in their 20s and 30s. We have incorporated prison ministry, and provided resources for the visually impaired.

The very core of all of these processes remains the same: to help people become better hearers and doers of the Word of God. We do this by encouraging and supporting the formation of small communities who gather prayerfully to reflect on and share the Word of God, to make better connections between faith and life, and to live their faith more concretely in family, work, and community life.

As a not-for-profit organization, our pastoral outreach is sustained in part from the sales of our publications and resources, and the stipends we receive for the services provided to parishes and dioceses. However, our priority is always to serve all parishes who desire to renew their faith and build the Church, regardless of their economic situation. We have been able to fulfill this mission not only in the inner city and rural areas in the United States, but also in the developing world, especially Latin America and Africa, thanks to donations and charitable funding.

As you meet in your small group, we invite you to take a few moments to imagine the great invisible network of others, here in the United States and on the other continents. They gather, as you do, in small Christian communities, around the Word of God present in the Scripture, striving to hear and act upon that Word. Keep them in your prayer: a prayer of thanksgiving for the many graces we have experienced; a prayer that the Spirit will guide all of us as we explore *Why Catholic?*

Introduction

Welcome to *Why Catholic? Journey through the Catechism.*

This four-book series was developed by RENEW International to provide a faith-sharing process for small communities, while unfolding the riches of the *Catechism of the Catholic Church* and the *United States Catholic Catechism for Adults*, both of which are published by the United States Conference of Catholic Bishops. By using these materials, we hope participants will be encouraged to study both catechisms in even greater depth, allowing the teachings within to illuminate their faith and promote an active response in love.

You are about to journey forward with *The Celebration of the Christian Mystery: Sacraments.* This book explores how we celebrate our faith in sacramental liturgy.

Why Catholic? is designed to highlight select teachings around which faith sharing may take place, rather than as a compendium or total summary of the catechisms. By nourishing and strengthening women and men in all callings, *Why Catholic?* can serve as an essential tool on the journey to mature Christian faith. We hope that the process will also enable participants to discover and embrace their own personal faith story and allow them to reflect on, and answer, the questions, "What does it mean to be Catholic? How did I become Catholic? Why do I remain Catholic?"

Why Catholic? is also designed to balance prayer, sharing on Scripture, and reflection on the teachings of our faith, providing a full and fruitful faith-sharing experience for participants. While a prayerful listening to and reflection on Scripture is an integral part of each session, *Why Catholic?* is not meant to be a Scripture study.

Why Catholic? is designed to correspond to the four pillars of the *Catechism of the Catholic Church* and its complement, the *United States Catholic Catechism for Adults.* The three other books in the *Why Catholic?* series are: *The Profession of Faith: What We Believe; Life in Christ: Walking with God;* and *Christian Prayer: Deepening My Experience of God.* If you are gathering in a small community, you may wish to meet either in two six-week blocks of time or during twelve consecutive weeks to allow one week per session.

In addition, we recommend participants keep a journal and, following each session, spend some time journaling key beliefs of the Catholic faith, along with their personal insights. The journal may serve as a valuable meditation tool as well as a springboard for sharing faith with others.

Throughout the *Why Catholic?* series, direct reference is made to both the *Catechism of the Catholic Church* and the *United States Catholic Catechism for Adults*. This material is identified as (*CCC*) and (*USCCA*) respectively. An excellent explanation of the relationship between the two catechisms can be found at the website of the United States Catholic Conference of Bishops: www.usccbpublishing.org/client/client_pdfs/Q&A_on_USCCA.pdf

We pray that your experience with *Why Catholic?* will lead to a closer, more vibrant relationship with our loving God and your community of faith.

Faith-Sharing Principles and Guidelines

When we gather as Christians to share our faith and grow together in community, it is important that we adhere to certain principles. The following Theological Principles and Small Community Guidelines will keep your community focused and help you to grow in faith, hope, and love.

Principles

- God leads each person on his or her spiritual journey. This happens in the context of the Christian community.

- Christ, the Word made flesh, is the root of Christian faith. It is because of Christ, and in and through him, that we come together to share our faith.

- Faith sharing refers to the shared reflections on the action of God in one's life experience as related to Scripture and the faith of the Church. Faith sharing is not discussion, problem solving, or Scripture study. The purpose is an encounter between a person in the concrete circumstances of his or her life and a loving God, leading to a conversion of heart.

- The entire faith-sharing process is an expression of prayerful reflection.

Guidelines

- Constant attention to respect, honesty, and openness for each person will assist the community's growth.

- Each person shares on the level where he or she feels comfortable.

- Silence is a vital part of the total process. Participants are given time to reflect before any sharing begins, and a period of comfortable silence might occur between individual sharings.

- Persons are encouraged to wait to share a second time until others who wish to do so have contributed.

- The entire community is responsible for participating and faith sharing.

- Confidentiality is essential, allowing each person to share honestly.
- Action flowing out of the small community meetings is essential for the growth of individuals and the community.

A Note to Small Community Leaders

Small Community Leaders are ...

- People who encourage participation and the sharing of our Christian faith.
- People who encourage the spiritual growth of the community and of its individual members through communal prayer, a prayerful atmosphere at meetings, and daily prayer and reflection on the Scriptures.
- People who move the community to action to be carried out between meetings. They are not satisfied with a self-centered comfort level in the community but are always urging that the faith of the community be brought to impact on their daily lives and the world around them.
- Community builders who create a climate of hospitality and trust among all participants.

Small Community Leaders are not ...

- Theologians: The nature of the meeting is faith sharing. Should a theological or scriptural question arise, the leader should turn to the pastor or staff to seek guidance.
- Counselors: The small communities are not intended for problem solving. This is an inappropriate setting to deal with emotionally laden issues of a personal nature. The leader is clearly not to enter the realm of treating people with emotional, in-depth feelings such as depression, anxiety, or intense anger. When someone moves in this direction, beyond faith sharing, the leader should bring the community back to faith sharing. With the help of the pastor or staff, the person should be advised to seek the assistance of professional counseling.
- Teachers: The leaders are not teachers. Their role is to guide the process of the faith sharing as outlined in the materials.

N.B. *SOWING SEEDS: Essentials for Small Community Leaders* provides a comprehensive collection of pastoral insights and practical suggestions to assist small community leaders in their crucial role of facilitating a *Why Catholic?* small community. Available from RENEW International's secure online webstore: www.renewintl.org/store

How to Use This Book

Whenever two or more of us gather in the name of Jesus, we are promised that Christ is in our midst (see Matthew 18:20). This book helps communities to reflect on the Scriptures, the *Catechism of the Catholic Church* and the *United States Catholic Catechism for Adults.* It is most helpful if some members of the group or the group as a whole have the Scriptures and one, or both, of the catechisms at their meeting.

Those who have met in small communities will be familiar with the process. In this book based on the *Catechism*, however, there is particular emphasis on the great mysteries of our faith. These reflections make demands upon our reflective nature and help in the formation of our Catholic values. **Therefore, it is important that participants carefully prepare for the session before coming to the meeting.** They are encouraged to read and reflect on the session itself, the Scripture passage(s) cited, and the sections or pages of the *CCC* and the *USCCA* referenced.

If the community has not met before or if participants do not know each other, take time for introductions and to get acquainted. People share most easily when they feel comfortable and accepted in a community.

Prayer must always be at the heart of our Christian gatherings. Following any necessary Introductions, sessions begin with a time of prayer—Lifting Our Hearts. There are suggested songs, but other appropriate songs may be used. All of the suggested songs are available on the *Songs for Faith Sharing on The Celebration of the Christian Mystery* CD, produced by RENEW International. See more details on page 97. Most of these songs can be found in the standard parish worship collections. If songs are copyright, remember you need to request permission before making copies of either the words or the music. The contact information for permissions can be found on page iv.

Each week, an action response— Living the Good News—is recommended. After the first week, the leader encourages participants to share how they put their faith in action by following through on their Living the Good News commitment from the previous session.

Following Lifting Our Hearts, and Living the Good News, there is an initial reflection on the *Catechism* entitled Reflection 1. The next section, Pondering the Word, offers a Scripture reference that one participant proclaims aloud from the Bible. Together, the *Catechism* and Scripture selections will give the community members the opportunity to reflect on what Jesus has said and to share their faith on the particular topic. Sharing could take about 15 minutes.

Next, the small community continues Reflection 2 and then considers the Sharing Our Faith questions. Faith-sharing groups vary greatly in their background and composition. In some sessions, the group may wish to start with the question: What insights into my faith did I gain from this session? Explain. Allow approximately 25 minutes for Sharing Our Faith, making sure the last question is always considered.

In coming to closure, each session offers some ideas for an individual or group action—Living the Good News. Here, participants reflect on how God is inviting them to act during the coming week—how to bring their faith into their daily lives. The ideas presented are merely suggestions. It is important that group members choose an action that is both measurable and realistic.

Each session then concludes with Lifting Our Hearts.

Sharing beyond the Small Community

As a community, you will be using this book as the focus for your sharing. You should consider how the fruits of your sharing can be taken beyond the confines of this group. For example, if you are parents, you could be asking what part of your faith exploration can be shared with your children. RENEW International has designed a resource, entitled RENEWING FAMILY FAITH, to help you achieve exactly this.

RENEWING FAMILY FAITH offers a two-page full-color bulletin for every session contained in the *Why Catholic?* faith-sharing books. You will find a full description of this invaluable resource on pages 96-97.

Suggested Format of the Sharing Sessions (1½ hours)

Introductions (when the group is new or when someone joins the group)

Lifting Our Hearts	10 minutes
Sharing the Good News	5 minutes
Reflection 1	10 minutes
Scripture: Pondering the Word and Sharing Question	15 minutes
Reflection 2	10 minutes
Sharing Our Faith	25 minutes
Living the Good News	10 minutes
Lifting Our Hearts	5 minutes

Liturgy:
Celebrating the Paschal Mystery

Suggested Environment

Bible, candle, and a small table on which a Bible may be enthroned. Consider decorating the table with colors of the liturgical year and other symbols of faith.

In addition it is suggested that the Catechism of the Catholic Church (CCC) *and the* United States Catholic Catechism for Adults (USCCA) *be available.*

Begin with a quiet, reflective atmosphere.

Lifting Our Hearts

Song Suggestion

"Gather Your People," Bob Hurd (OCP)

Prayer

Pray together

God our Father,
through you Son, Jesus Christ,
you call us in this moment
to sing your praise
and further your reign
in relationship with others
through the guidance and inspiration
of your Holy Spirit.

How you do this is a mystery,
we do not fully understand.

We bow in thankfulness and praise
as we reflect on the mystery of your love for us.

Give us new light to see the depths
of your guidance and inspiration in our daily lives.

Send your Holy Spirit into our hearts and minds
that we might search out the signs of the times
and answer the needs of our world.

Grant us the grace to give witness to your presence
and your love among us.

Bless us as we gather as disciples of Jesus Christ,
your Son and our Lord. Amen.

Spotlight on the *Catechism*

"A mystery is a reality that is both visible and hidden. Jesus Christ's death and Resurrection become present to us and effective for us in the liturgical life of the Church. His death and Resurrection are hidden now in the eternity of God, but as Risen Lord and Head of the Church, Jesus Christ calls us to share in them through the liturgy of the Church, that is, by the visible gathering of the community for worship and remembrance of what God has done for us."

United States Catholic Catechism for Adults, p. 167

Reflection 1

Celebrating our faith

The Easter Vigil liturgy began once night had truly fallen. Instead of processing into the church behind the newly lit paschal candle, the people were already gathered inside. My wife and four daughters were squeezed into a pew at the front of the darkened church. With the rest of the faithful, we followed the celebrant with our eyes as he walked back to the double doors and threw them open. From a huge cloud of incense the lighted paschal candle emerged, held aloft by the deacon. We nudged my daughters out into the central aisle for a better view. Wide-eyed, three-year-old Una (who had just celebrated her birthday) watched the simple rite unfold. Before the deacon launched into the *Exsultet*, Una began to sing, *"Happy birthday to you ..."* Those who could hear her, and in the silence of the church there were many, were neither offended nor distracted. They smiled in recognition of, and perhaps in longing for, the natural spontaneity with which the little voice welcomed the light of the risen Christ.

Each year at the Easter Vigil, a new paschal candle is lit symbolizing "the light of Christ, rising in glory, scattering the darkness of our hearts and minds" (*Built of Living Stones*, 94). In the light of the paschal candle, the deacon sings the *Exsultet*, an ancient hymn that proclaims the risen Christ and places his Paschal Mystery—his life, death, resurrection, and glorification—within the context of God's plan for salvation for all.

"Paschal Mystery" is the term used to designate the life, death, resurrection, and glorification of Jesus. Christ lived, died, is risen from the dead and has returned in glory to his Father—not just for himself but for all God's creation. This is the mystery that established the new covenant with humanity. This is such Good News for us that we, like Una, cannot stop ourselves from celebrating it! As Catholics, we enter into this new covenant primarily through the liturgy and the sacraments. In this first session of *The Celebration of Christian Mystery: Sacraments*, we look to the importance of liturgy in our lives and reflect on the reality that liturgy celebrates, namely, the Paschal Mystery of Jesus.

The word "paschal" comes from the Hebrew word for "passing over." The Book of Exodus tells us that God sent a series of plagues upon the Egyptians when Pharaoh refused to release the Hebrew slaves. The tenth plague was to kill the first-born male of every family, including Pharaoh's own son. God instructed the Israelites to sacrifice a lamb and sprinkle their doorposts with its blood. The angel of the Lord would then pass over the homes of the Israelites and their first-born sons would be saved. After they had fled and were wandering in the wilderness, Pharaoh sent his army after them. The Lord told Moses to raise his staff and the Red Sea parted allowing the Israelites to pass over onto dry land. After they had crossed, the waters returned, the army was destroyed, and Israel was no longer an enslaved people.

When we think of the word "mystery" we tend to think of a puzzle or fictional story in which a detective seeks to solve a crime. The emphasis is on what is *not* known. In the New Testament, mystery means using what we know to glimpse at what is beyond knowing. St. Paul captured this sense of mystery when he said, "For now we see in a mirror, dimly, but then we will see face to face. Now I know only in part; then I will know fully, even as I have been fully known" (1 Corinthians 13:12).

For Christians the Paschal Mystery is Christ's passing through death to resurrection and returning to the Father. The sacraments draw us into the unfolding truth of God's salvation, inviting and enabling us share in the death of Christ so that we too can share in his resurrection and glory. "Through the liturgical celebrations of the Church, we participate in the Paschal Mystery of Christ, that is, his passing through death from this life into eternal glory, just as God enabled the people of ancient Israel to pass from slavery to freedom through the events narrated in the Book of Exodus (cf. Exodus 11-13). The liturgies of the Church also help to teach us about Jesus Christ and the meaning of the mysteries we are celebrating" (*USCAA*, p. 167).

Liturgy is primarily the prayer of Christ and of his Church to the Father. "The word 'liturgy' originally meant a 'public work' or a 'service in the name of/on behalf of the people.' In Christian tradition, it means the participation of the People of God in 'the work of God (cf. John 17:4)" (*CCC*, 1069). In liturgy, we not only offer praise to God we also proclaim the Gospel and hear its call to live out that Gospel in our daily lives. As Church, we share in Christ's threefold gift to his Church of teaching, sanctifying, and shepherding his people (*CCC*, 1070).

Liturgy is the official public prayer of the Church. "The liturgy is the summit toward which the activity of the Church is directed; at the same time it is the font from which all the Church's power flows" (*Sacrosanctum concilium*, 10). In liturgy we express and experience ourselves as Church and, at the same time, constitute ourselves as Church. Over time, the liturgy both forms us as disciples of Christ and shapes the way we live our lives. When we enter fully into liturgical celebrations, our lives become integrated with our faith, and we enter more consciously and more fully into Christ's Paschal Mystery in life's daily experiences.

"As the work of Christ liturgy is also an action of his *Church*" (*CCC*, 1071). Liturgy makes the Church present as a visible sign of the communion between God and us as human beings. Even more, the liturgy is an instrument of the Church. "It engages the faithful in the new life of the community and involves the 'conscious, active, and fruitful participation' of everyone (*Sacrosanctum concilium*, 11)" (*CCC*, 1071). We are invited and called to enter liturgical worship with our whole selves, with all our minds, bodies, hearts, and souls because this is a privileged place where we meet Christ and where we find new life.

Remember the paschal candle, symbol of the risen Christ. Notice how during the Easter Season, the paschal candle remains in the sanctuary. After the Easter season, it is moved to the baptistery for use in the celebration of baptisms. During funerals it is placed near the casket as "a sign of the Christian's passover from death to life" (*Built of Living Stones*, 94, citing *[Circular Letter Concerning] the Preparation and Celebration of the Easter Feasts*, no. 99). From baptism until our own dying to this life we are caught up in the Paschal Mystery—the life, death, and resurrection of Jesus—as we follow him in response to his living invitation.

Listen attentively to as Paul describes what the Paschal Mystery means for us his Letter to the Romans.

Pondering the Word

Dying and Rising with Christ

Romans 6:3-11

Take a few minutes to savor a word, a phrase, a question, or a feeling that rises up in you. Reflect on this quietly or share it aloud.

Sharing Question

• How in my own life is the Paschal Mystery—the life, death and resurrection of Jesus—present?

Reflection 2

Liturgy is Trinitarian

The ultimate aim of liturgy is "the perfect glorification of God and the sanctification of those who celebrate it" (*Sacrosanctum concilium*, 7). God does not need us to tell him he is great. We need to give glory to God to be human. Creation exists so that God can give God's self to it. This gift is love. Liturgy is an encounter between the faithful and God where we, both as a body and as individual members, enter into the presence of the triune God. God's creation itself reveals God's power and providence and, in this, gives glory. Even more, God's desire to be united to creation and his faithful care of his creatures disclose a God who is as personal as he is powerful, as concerned as he is creative. In the liturgy we acknowledge God the powerful, God the personal. Even more, we acknowledge that God is three persons—Father, Son, Spirit.

"Liturgy is centered on the Holy Trinity. At every liturgy the action of worship is directed to the Father, from whom all blessings come, through the Son in the unity of the Holy Spirit" (*USCCA*, p. 167). The Father is the origin and end of all creation and salvation. Jesus Christ the Son of God, the Word Made Flesh, who is the sacrament who reveals and makes present the Father. He is the mediator who in his person unites humankind with God. The Holy Spirit is the personal power of God, enabling Christ to be present in our midst, lifting and bringing us to the Father. In liturgy we are drawn into the life of the

Trinity. God reaches out to us through the Son in the Spirit. In response, we in the liturgy praise the Father through the Son in the Spirit.

For example, the Eucharistic Prayers are addressed to the Father. They are an expression of the mediation of Jesus Christ. Each Eucharistic Prayer calls upon the power of the Holy Spirit to come upon the people and the sacramental elements so that Christ can be present in the here and now. All liturgy is about making memory but in a special way. We do not just remember a past event; we also celebrate the presence in our assembly of a particular aspect of the Paschal Mystery. In the liturgy the Paschal Mystery is made present. Even more, it makes it real and effective in the lives of those who take part in the celebration. It is in the presence of the Paschal Mystery that God's love of union and of faithful care is disclosed. In the power of that presence we are enabled to unite ourselves to Christ and, through him, to his Father. Because Christ has joined us, even joining us in death, and sends the Spirit upon us, we are able to join him and return to the Father.

Sharing Our Faith

• How is my participation in liturgy "conscious, active, and fruitful"?

• What are the obstacles to my active participation in the liturgy?

Living the Good News

Determine a specific action (individual or group) that flows from your sharing. This should be your primary consideration for choosing an action.

If choosing an individual action, determine what you will do and share it with the group. If choosing a group action, determine who will take responsibility for different aspects of the action.

The following are secondary suggestions:

• Read and reflect on the Scripture readings for the coming Sunday to prepare for the Eucharistic Liturgy.

• Become more conscious of your responses at the liturgy.

• Visit the United States Conference of Catholic Bishops website on the new English translation of the *Roman Missal*, www.usccb.org/romanmissal

In light of this session, this week I commit to:

As a group pray for each Member by Name.

Joyce Maggie Carol Pat Thelda Ellen Me. Alice

Lifting Our Hearts

Invite one person to take the leader's part. All pray the response together.

Response	**Renew your Church, O God.**
Leader	Help us to bring our entire lives to the liturgical gathering. *Response*
Leader	Jesus, help us to be mindful that your Church is made up of people who are broken and need healing: *Response*
Leader	Remind us often that whatever we do to others, we do to you: *Response*
Leader	Give us the strength to reach out to help those in need: *Response*
Leader	Help us to love as you love us: *Response*
Leader	O Father, let the entire world know of your love: *Response*
Leader	O Holy Spirit, renew your Church As the sacrament of salvation: *Response*
All	**Father in heaven, we present these petitions to you and all those that still rest quietly in our hearts.**
	Call upon your Spirit to fill us with the gifts we need to live in you more fully today.
	We ask this through Christ our Lord. Amen.

Looking Ahead

- Prepare for your next session by prayerfully reading and studying:
  - Session 2: Sacraments: Signs of the New Covenant;
  - Scripture: Luke 24:28-35;
  - pages 165-168 from Chapter 14, "The Celebration of the Paschal Mystery of Christ," from the *United States Catholic Catechism for Adults;*
  - paragraphs 1076-1112 of the *Catechism of the Catholic Church.*
- Remember to use *Renewing Family Faith* and its helpful suggestions on how to extend the fruits of your sharing beyond your group, especially to your families (see pages 96-97).

Sacraments:
Signs of the New Covenant

Suggested Environment

Bible, candle, and a small table on which a Bible may be enthroned. Consider decorating the table with symbols of the sacraments such as water, oil, a stole, bread, and wine.

In addition it is suggested that the Catechism of the Catholic Church (CCC) *and the* United States Catholic Catechism for Adults (USCCA) *be available.*

Begin with a quiet, reflective atmosphere.

Lifting Our Hearts

Song Suggestion
"Amazing Grace," John Newton (Public domain)

④

Prayer

Response	**We thank you, God, our Father.**
Leader	For feeding us and healing us, for forgiving us and bringing us together in the sacraments of your Church: *Response*
Leader	For all the wonders of the earth, for green mountains and blue skies, for blue-green oceans and brown deserts: *Response*
Leader	For the gift of life that comes to us in the sacraments: *Response*
Leader	For the wonderful ways you nurture us by Christ's action in the sacraments of the Church: *Response*

Leader   We thank you, Father, with your Son and Spirit.
              Amen.

All   **God gives us what we need.**
              God's love endures forever. Amen.

Sharing Our Good News

The leader invites members of the group to share how they lived the Good News since their last meeting.

Reflection 1

Grace

I almost didn't go. I had lots of reasons to stay home and not join the family for Thanksgiving that year. And besides, we did it every year. Just once, they wouldn't miss me. The price of fuel was up and I was already on a tight budget. No, this year I'd stay home and have dinner with friends close by. It was settled.

> # Spotlight on the *Catechism*
>
> "Jesus gave us the Sacraments to call us to worship God, to build up the Church, to deepen our faith, to show us how to pray, to connect us with the living Tradition of the Church, and to sanctify us. While God works primarily through the Sacraments, he also touches us through the community of the Church, through the lives of holy people, through prayer, spirituality and acts of love."
>
> *United States Catholic Catechism for Adults*, p. 170

That was Monday. Tuesday night after supper I got into a cleaning mood and tackled the bookcase in the living room. One by one, I emptied the shelves, dusted, wiped off each book and put it back. When I reached the bottom shelf, I sat on the floor and worked on until I picked up a photo album I'd created, and started leafing through it. It was late, I was tired, and it was relaxing to just enjoy remembering one event after another.

About half way through the album, I came to pages of photos from a Thanksgiving dinner several years ago. There were photos of people arriving, hugs and kisses, a table laden with food, my family huddled close together, and bowing our heads as we gave thanks. One photo really touched me: three family members who were no longer with us. This year two new babies I hadn't yet met would be there, and that got me thinking.

The weather was bad, the traffic was heavy, and the 200 miles seemed like an endless journey, but I was on my way. I was on my way because I would miss them and all Thanksgiving has come to mean to me and my family over the years. We hugged and kissed, and gathered around the table we gave thanks for all we are and all we have. Afterwards the babies slept, we cleaned up. Some went out in the yard for the traditional football game, some stayed in and chatted. I was with my family again. And to think I almost didn't go. I almost thought they wouldn't miss me. I almost thought I wouldn't miss them!

Thanksgiving Day is really an American holy day. It offers us a time to come to a table of plenty, to share our bounty, to tell family stories, to express gratitude for our gifts, to celebrate who we have become. As Catholics in the United States come to their Thanksgiving Day table, Catholics of the world come to the table of the Lord to share in God's bounty, to hear told the stories of their family of faith, to acknowledge gratefully God's gifts to them, to celebrate who they have become.

In session one, we explored the meaning of the Paschal Mystery and how that mystery is made present and effective in the celebration of the liturgy. This session will focus on the sacraments, the most important liturgical actions. "Liturgy" and "sacraments" are not identical terms. "The term *liturgy* … embraces all the official public prayer life of the Church, while the term *Sacrament* refers to a particular celebration of Christ's salvific work" (*USCCA*, pp. 167-168). The Church teaches that Jesus Christ our Lord instituted the sacraments and that "[t]he saving words and deeds of Jesus Christ are the foundation of what he would communicate in the Sacraments through the ministers of the Church" (*USCCA*, p. 168).

Catholics speak of seven "sacraments": Baptism, Confirmation, Eucharist, Penance, Anointing of the Sick, Holy Orders, and Matrimony. In the Church's earliest days, these ritualized prayers were not called "sacraments" but "mysteries." This was the case because through them we perceive and are drawn into the Paschal Mystery of the life, death, resurrection, and glorification of Jesus Christ. "Mystery," derived from Greek, and "sacrament," derived from Latin, actually refer to the same reality; what we in the Latin Church call "sacraments," the Eastern Churches still refer to as mysteries.

 "Sacraments are 'powers that come forth' from the Body of Christ (cf. Luke 5:17, 6:19, 8:46), which is ever-living and life-giving. They are actions of the Holy Spirit at work in his Body, the Church. They are the 'masterworks of God' in the new and everlasting covenant" (*CCC*, 1116). Throughout history, God has chosen unique ways to love us and to show us that love. In the Covenant with Moses, the Chosen People commemorated their relationship with God through "circumcision, anointing and consecration of kings and priests, laying on of hands, sacrifices, and above all the Passover" (*CCC*, 1150). Even more than signs, these were effective signs: They not only recalled and pointed to God's action, they acknowledged God's presence among them.

"The Church sees in these signs a prefiguring of the sacraments of the New Covenant" (*CCC*, 1150), mediated by Jesus Christ. Because of who we are and how we are, we need to feel and experience God's love in concrete, visible ways. The sacraments are visible, concrete signs of God's loving relationship with us, as well as instruments through which our lives are transformed into the likeness of Christ. "The invisible reality we cannot 'see' is God's grace, his gracious initiative in redeeming us through the death and Resurrection of his Son" (*USCCA*, p. 168).

> # Spotlight on the *Catechism*
>
> "… for believers the sacraments of the New Covenant are *necessary for salvation* (cf. Council of Trent [1547]: DS 1604)…. The fruit of the sacramental life is that the Spirit of adoption makes the faithful partakers in the divine nature (cf. 2 Peter 1:4)"
>
> *Catechism of the Catholic Church*, 1129

A sacrament is a sign, which shows forth something, and also an instrument, which makes something present. In terms of "showing forth/making present" God's activity, we can see that the term "sacrament" is not limited to the seven sacraments of the Church. "Sacrament" can also refer to Christ and also to his Church. It is in Christ that we experience God's love in the most visible way and that the presence and power of God is made present. This is why we call Christ the "primordial sacrament." Jesus Christ is the sacrament of encounter with God. In him, God's saving activity and our grateful worship are shown forth and made present in human history.

The seven sacraments are signs and instruments of the "primitive" sacrament of the Church, showing forth and making the Church of Christ present and operative. Moreover, the seven sacraments are actions of Christ and of his Church. "Christ now acts through the sacraments he instituted to communicate his grace. The sacraments are perceptible signs (words and actions) accessible to our human nature. By the action of Christ and the power of the Holy Spirit they make present efficaciously the grace that they signify" (*CCC*, 1084). When a priest baptizes a baby, the Church is active and Christ is active. When the Eucharist is celebrated, the action is not only Christ's but the Church's, and the resultant communion is not only with

Christ but also with the Church. When the sacrament of penance is celebrated, the action and extension of forgiveness is not only that of Christ; it is also the action of the forgiveness of the body of Christ, the Church.

The fruit of the encounter with Christ and with his Church in the sacraments is grace. Very simply, grace is a freely bestowed gift of God, an active expression of God's love for us, a share in the very life of God. Through grace, God becomes present to us, and this presence really and truly changes us, recreating us in the image of the Son. Even our response to grace is a gift of grace. God enables us to accept who we have become and empowers us to live new and holy lives (*CCC*, 1989, 1966). God's gracious gift changes us down to our socks, and enables us to be signs and instruments of God's presence and power in the circumstances of our lives and throughout our world.

Pondering the Word

Their Eyes Were Opened

Luke 24:28-35

Take a few minutes to savor a word, a phrase, a question, or a feeling that rises up in you. Reflect on this quietly or share it aloud.

Sharing Question

• When did I, like the disciples on the road to Emmaus, recognize God's grace in my life?

Reflection 2

The Sacramental Principle

What makes Catholicism catholic? Some say it is the sacramental principle, the notion that all reality, both animate and inanimate, is potentially or in fact the bearer of God's presence and the instrument of God's saving activity on behalf of humanity. This principle is rooted in the nature of a sacrament as a visible sign of the invisible presence and activity of God. "God speaks to man through the visible creation.... Light and darkness, wind and fire, water and earth, the tree and its fruit speak of God and symbolize both his greatness and his nearness" (*CCC*, 1147). Together with the principles of mediation (God works through secondary agents to achieve divine ends) and communion (the end of all God's activity is the unity of humanity), the principle of sacramentality constitutes one of the central theological characteristics of Catholicism.

The seven sacraments are privileged encounters with Christ. The word "sacrament" is derived from the Latin word "sacramentum" (derived from the root *sacer,* referring to that which makes something sacred). In ancient Rome, a sacramentum was the military oath that a Roman soldier swore to his legion or emperor.

The first three sacraments—Baptism, Confirmation, and Eucharist— are sacraments of initiation; they "lay the *foundations* of every Christian life" (*CCC,* 1212). Penance and the Anointing of the Sick are sacraments of healing; in these the Church continues Jesus Christ's "work of healing and salvation, even among her own members" (*CCC,* 1421). Holy Orders and Matrimony are the sacraments at the service of communion and the mission of the faithful; they "are directed towards the salvation of others" (*CCC,* 1534).

"A sacramental celebration is woven from signs and symbols … [T]heir meaning is rooted in the work of creation and in human culture, specified by the events of the Old Covenant and fully revealed in the person and work of Christ" (*CCC,* 1145). Symbols contain and reveal the presence of Christ and the Paschal Mystery. A sign, like a stop sign at a corner, sets out information; it has one meaning. Symbols do more than point to or stand for another reality; that reality is revealed in the structure of the symbol.

Consider the symbolism of bread and wine. Bread does not just happen; it is the result of a long process of development. Grain is crushed, milled, water (baptism) is added, it has to rise, be kneaded, and baked (by the Spirit). Wine does not just happen; it must sit for a long time if it is going to ferment properly, like us if we are going to become a source of life (blood) for others. In their very

Spotlight on the *Catechism*

"The Church celebrates the liturgy using an abundance of signs, symbols, and rituals. We celebrate the Sacraments with scriptural readings, homilies, music, processions, blessings, bread, wine, oil, arms outstretched in prayer, gestures of peace, bowed heads, kneeling, standing, sitting, incense, holy water, flowers, candles, colors, ritual vestments, choirs and musical instruments….Since the Son of God honored us by becoming incarnate—the true visible image of the invisible God—we use these signs and symbols to help us experience God's invisible presence"

United States Catholic Catechism for Adults, p. 171

structures, bread and wine reveal something of the reality of our call to become the body of Christ.

Basic symbolic actions in the liturgy include making the sign of the cross, taking holy water, kneeling, and folding hands. To express one's self symbolically means to let appear on the outside what is happening on the inside. In Baptism, water is poured on the head of a person; it symbolizes the washing of the body. The rite of Baptism signifies the cleansing of a person's soul of sin and the beginning of new life in Christ. Because the rite is a sacrament, instituted by Christ, it is the action of Christ. To think and act symbolically is to recognize how outwards signs express an inner conviction.

A symbol is the smallest unit of any ritual. Ritual trains us in how to be rather than mirroring our feelings. As individuals, we do not form the rite; the rite forms us. The sacraments "nourish, strengthen, and express" our faith (*CCC*, 1123). According to the ancient saying, *lex orandi, lex credendi,* the church believes as she prays. In celebrating the sacraments, the Church "confesses the faith received from the apostles" (*CCC*, 1124). Ritual forms us, and when regularly repeated its power to transform us can be more and more fully realized. In the liturgy, particularly the sacraments, we encounter Christ, enter into his Paschal Mystery, and are transformed.

Sharing Our Faith

- Think of a time when you noticed the sacramental principle at work in your life. Where were you? What were you doing? Share with the group.
- When I participate in the Sunday liturgy, what are my favorite symbolic actions? Why? What do the symbolic actions mean?
- What has helped me to experience the grace of the sacraments?
- What are some practical ways in which I can dispose myself to accept the gift of grace more easily (weekend retreat, Sunday drive, lunch-hour prayer)?

Living the Good News

Determine a specific action (individual or group) that flows from your sharing. This should be your primary consideration for choosing an action.

If choosing an individual action, determine what you will do and share it with the group. If choosing a group action, determine who will take responsibility for different aspects of the action.

The following are secondary suggestions:

- Participate fully in the sacrament of Eucharist this week paying special attention to the symbolic actions of the presider and the assembly. Prepare for this by taking some reflective time.

- Share with members of your family how God has worked in your life through the sacraments. Invite one family member to join you in a celebration of the Eucharistic liturgy or Penance and Reconciliation this week.

- Reflect upon your role as a godparent, confirmation sponsor, or attendant at someone's marriage. Pray for and reach out to your godson or goddaughter, the confirmand, or the couple this week.

In light of this session, this week I commit to:

_____

_____

Lifting Our Hearts

Offer spontaneous prayers of gratitude for the sacraments.

To conclude, sing the first verse of "Amazing Grace."

Looking Ahead

- Prepare for your next session by prayerfully reading and studying:
  - Session 3: The Body of Christ at Prayer;
  - Scripture: 1 Corinthians 12:4-12, 27-31;
  - Chapter 10: "The Church: Reflecting the Light of Christ" (pages 111-123) and pages 170-171, "Liturgy is the Body of Christ at Prayer," in Chapter 14 in the *United States Catholic Catechism for Adults;*
  - paragraphs 1113-1144 from the *Catechism of the Catholic Church.*
- Remember to use RENEWING FAMILY FAITH and its helpful suggestions on how to extend the fruits of your sharing beyond your group, especially to your families (see pages 96-97).

The Body of Christ at Prayer

Bible, candle, and a small table on which a Bible may be enthroned. Consider decorating the table with colors of the liturgical year and other symbols of faith.

In addition it is suggested that the Catechism of the Catholic Church (CCC) *and the* United States Catholic Catechism for Adults (USCCA) *be available.*

Begin with a quiet, reflective atmosphere.

Lifting Our Hearts

Song Suggestion

"Come to the Table," Tony Galla (White Dove/OCP/RENEW)

Prayer

Leader	We thank You, God of Mysterious Ways, that You have a holy design for each of us.
Side 1	We rejoice that we are, each of us, Special to You, that our names are written in the palm of Your hand and our place in history, our purpose for existing, is known within Your heart, since endless ages.
Side 2	We are grateful for that long line of holy people, who since ancient times have inspired others by their faithfulness to their own special destinies.

They, by their very lives
shout out to us
not to compromise our destinies,
but to live fully within Your eternal design.

Side 1   Blessed are You, Inscrutable Lord,
for those events, persons, talents, and loves
which have helped us to discover
adventure and purpose,
fruitfulness and meaning,
in our sometimes empty
and seemingly insignificant lives.

Side 2   Blessed are You
for teachers, parents, and other guides
who call us out
from the cocoon of comfort and contentment
to embark upon that unique path
which You have set forth
for each of Your sons and daughters.

All   **Blessed are You, Lord our God,**
who has given to each of us
a personal destiny and purpose in life. Amen.

("Blessed Are You, Lord Our God, Who Has Given to Each of Us a Personal Destiny and Purpose in Life," Prayers for the Domestic Church by Edward Hays)

Sharing Our Good News

The leader invites members of the group to share how they lived the Good News since their last meeting.

Reflection 1

We are the Body of Christ

Dorothy Day spent her life among the poor. As a journalist she was committed to exposing injustice and the plight of the poor. She led a Bohemian lifestyle among literary and progressive political circles until she joined the Roman Catholic Church. Following her conversion, she began publishing a newspaper called *The Catholic Worker,* which was initially directed at the unemployed during the Depression. *The Catholic Worker* examined the social issues of the day in light of the prophets of Israel, the Gospels, the teaching of the Church Fathers, and the social encyclicals of the popes. She believed that being a part of the "brotherhood of man and the Fatherhood of God" meant addressing such issues as labor unions, race, hunger, and housing. She also put her ideas into action by opening "Houses of Hospitality" where the hungry were fed and the homeless were housed. She could see Christ in the men and women who came looking for food, a drink, a place to sleep or just rest. She helped the poor and she also chose poverty for herself. She believed that to love the poor, one becomes like them.

The previous two sessions have focused on the underlying meaning of the liturgy and the sacraments, which is the celebration of the Paschal Mystery. This session answers the question: Who celebrates liturgy? "Liturgy is an 'action' of the *whole Christ* (*Christus totus*)" (*CCC*, 1136). Whereas Christ is the "principal celebrant," all celebrate the liturgy as part of the Body of Christ, which we belong to through our Baptism.

The Body of Christ has two different but essential meanings. The first meaning is about the presence of Jesus in the Eucharist. Through the celebration of the Eucharist, bread and wine is transformed into the Body and Blood of Christ. When we receive Communion, the eucharistic minister says, "The Body of Christ." We respond, "Amen." A second meaning refers to all those who enjoy communion with one another as a result of their baptism and faith. Paul's use of "Body of Christ" referred to those who were baptized *and* also to the Eucharist. He and the early Christians were not confused by the two meanings. Christian life is not about merely receiving the Body of Christ; it is about *being* the Body of Christ.

In this second meaning, the Body of Christ is understood as a community of people who profess faith in Jesus and whose members combine their individual gifts to work together to make Jesus alive and present in the world. As a central part of the Body of Christ, the church, through its words and actions, is to carry on Jesus' work of building the reign of God. It is our

Spotlight on the *Catechism*

"Mother Church earnestly desires that all the faithful should be led to that full, conscious, and active participation in liturgical celebrations which is demanded by the very nature of the liturgy, and to which the Christian people, 'a chosen race, a royal priesthood, a holy nation, a redeemed people,' have a right and an obligation by reason of their Baptism."

Sacrosanctum concilium, 14;
cf. 1 Peter 2:9; 2:4-5
Catechism of the Catholic Church, 1141

task to remind all the world's people that we have a common center—Jesus Christ, and that we are one dignified whole. We are an ongoing reminder that all the world has been saved by Jesus.

"In the unity of this Body [of which Christ is the head], there is a diversity of members and functions. All members are linked to one another, especially to those who are suffering, to the poor and persecuted" (CCC, 806). Dorothy Day had a special understanding of her relationship to the poor in the Body of Christ.

Because liturgical celebrations are public, not private, functions, they "pertain to the whole Body of the Church. They manifest it, and have effects upon it" (CCC, 1140, quoting *Sacrosanctum concilium*, 26). The sacraments bring people into the Body of Christ and keep them connected to the Body of Christ, as this is manifest in the church, whose mission it is to carry on the work of Christ in the world.

In the sacramental ritual of the Eucharist, bread is transformed into the Body of Christ. Bread is taken, blessed, broken, and shared with the people to be eaten. The faithful are reminded that they are the Body of Christ and, as with the bread, they too are to be taken, blessed, broken, and shared with others.

Spotlight on the *Catechism*

"The entire Body of Christ, animated by the Holy Spirit, celebrates the liturgy. The celebrating assembly is the community of the baptized. Liturgy is not a matter of private prayer, but a public act of worship by the faithful gathered together by the power of the Spirit under the authority of the bishop, their teacher and shepherd."

United States Catholic Catechism for Adults, p. 170

"In every liturgical action the Holy Spirit is sent in order to bring us into communion with Christ and so to form his Body" (CCC, 1108). It is by the power of the Holy Spirit that we are brought into union with Christ and one another, thus forming one body. It is the Spirit who brings us into full communion with the divine persons of the Trinity as well as with our fellow Christians. It is the Spirit that makes the gift of communion bear fruit. Through the power of the Holy Spirit, we can carry the Good News to the world. "Christ's work in the liturgy is sacramental: because his mystery of salvation is made present there by the power of his Holy Spirit; because his Body, which is the Church, is like a sacrament (sign and instrument) in which the Holy Spirit dispenses the mystery of salvation; and because through her liturgical actions the pilgrim Church already participates, as by a foretaste in the heavenly liturgy" (*CCC*, 1111).

Pondering the Word

One Body, Many Parts

1 Corinthians 12:4-12, 27-31

Take a few minutes to savor a word, a phrase, a question, or a feeling that rises up in you. Reflect on this quietly or share it aloud.

Sharing Questions

• What does it mean for me to be a member of the Body of Christ?

• What does it mean for me to "break the bread" of my own life for the sake of other?

Reflection 2

United in Christ

The Lord has given us, the members of the body of Christ, a variety of gifts that are activated by the Holy Spirit. In the Church there are apostles, prophets, and teachers; but not everyone can be an apostle, prophet, or teacher. Together we are the Body of Christ, and individually we are members of the Body of Christ. As we grow in faith we, along with the community, discern our gifts and our roles as individual members. But we are always united in Christ for the Church "is 'the sacrament of unity' … the holy people united and organized under the authority of the bishops" (*CCC*, 1140, quoting *Sacrosanctum concilium*, 26). In the liturgy, as one body of Christ, we offer our prayer to the Father.

When we celebrate liturgy, it "is the whole community, the Body of Christ united with its Head, that celebrates" (*CCC*, 1140). However, "the members do not all have the same function" (Romans 12:4). "Certain members are called by God, in and through the Church, to a special service of the community. These servants are chosen and consecrated by the sacrament of Holy Orders, by which the Holy Spirit enables them to act in the person of Christ the head, for the service of all the members of the Church (cf. PO 2;15)" (*CCC*, 1142). As Catholics, we believe that in the celebration of the liturgy and the sacraments, the ordained priest acts in the person of Christ. This means that the ordained priest speaks and acts in the name of Jesus and with the special authority of Jesus in his role as president-leader of liturgy.

While the ordained minister presides at the sacrament, every member of the baptized has a function within the celebration of the sacraments. All members of the body of Christ participate in the common priesthood of Christ. Every person who has been baptized into the body of Christ is called to share in the threefold function of Jesus as of teaching, leading and sanctifying. Some are called to particular ministries, not as ordained priests but to assist the common priesthood of the faithful. These include lectors, cantors, servers, and extraordinary ministers of holy Communion. So the entire assembly celebrates, each according to his or her own function (See *CCC*, 1143).

As a member of the assembly, there are many ways each of us can actively participate in the celebration. Sometimes we have become so familiar with the liturgy that our presence and our responses are automatic and lack focus. Coming to the liturgy after having prayed and shared about the Scriptures ahead of time is attentive commitment. When we come to church, we greet others as true sisters and brothers; we recognize that we are gathering as a community, not as an amalgam of individuals. When the celebrant asks for our response, we respond enthusiastically. We sing; we need to be conscious of what we are doing.

As individual members of the larger Body of Christ, we are called to sit at the table of the Lord, to share in his life and to be transformed. Ultimately, this transformation allows others to experience God through us. In other words, we become sacraments for others.

Sharing Our Faith

- How do I participate in sacramental liturgy? Am I more an active participant or an observer? Why?

- How fully do I embrace the communal element of celebrating the sacraments, both during the celebration and after I have gone back to daily life?

- What can I do differently that will allow my participation in liturgy to be fruitful in the world?

Living the Good News

Determine a specific action (individual or group) that flows from your sharing. This should be your primary consideration for choosing an action.

If choosing an individual action, determine what you will do and share it with the group. If choosing a group action, determine who will take responsibility for different aspects of the action.

The following are secondary suggestions:

As a member of the Church, determine to help others increase or strengthen their faith:

- Prepare before liturgy by praying for the larger Body of Christ of which you are part.

- Make a commitment to pray the Liturgy of the Hours this week to carry praying with the Body of Christ into daily life.

- Speak to the pastor about forming a hospitality committee to help welcome new people before each Mass.

In light of this session, this week I commit to:

_____

_____

Lifting Our Hearts

First, offer spontaneous prayer. Then pray together:

Jesus, our model,
Help us to know how to serve
and be served.

Help us to become servants of one another.

Give us wholeness and holiness in our days,
and bless us with the awareness
of the good we can accomplish
through the power of the Holy Spirit.

Remove all taint of self-centeredness from our hearts.

Give us joy when we serve —
humility when we are served.

Let us feel your love through one another.

Let those who serve and those who are served
bestow on one another
a deeper taste of the Spirit's peace. Amen.

Looking Ahead

- Prepare for your next session by prayerfully reading and studying:
  - Session 4: Baptism: Born to New Life in Christ;
  - Scripture: Matthew 3:13-17;
  - Chapter 15: "Baptism: Becoming a Christian," pages 181-199 in the *United States Catholic Catechism for Adults;*
  - paragraphs 1213-1284 of the *Catechism of the Catholic Church.*
- Remember to use RENEWING FAMILY FAITH and its helpful suggestions on how to extend the fruits of your sharing beyond your group, especially to your families (see pages 96-97).

Baptism:
Born to New Life in Christ

Suggested Environment

Bible, candle, and a small table on which a Bible may be enthroned. Consider decorating the table with colors of the liturgical year and symbols of Baptism such as water, a candle, oil, white robe, etc.

In addition it is suggested that the Catechism of the Catholic Church (CCC) *and the* United States Catholic Catechism for Adults (USCCA) *be available.*

Begin with a quiet, reflective atmosphere.

Lifting Our Hearts

Song Suggestion

"I Give My Life," Michael Semana and Norma Catherine (White Dove/OCP/RENEW)

Prayer

Pray together

Dear Father,
We gather this day in gratitude
For eternal life: to know you, the one true God,
and Jesus Christ, whom you have sent.
Christ has been raised from the dead
and appointed by God as the Lord of life
and ruler of all things, seen and unseen.
Help us to grow as his disciples and members of his church,
to be guided to the fullness of the truth
that he has revealed to us,
to make the mind of Christ Jesus our own,
to strive to pattern our lives on the teachings of the Gospel
and so to love the Lord our God and our neighbor.

For this was Christ's command
and he was its perfect example.
We ask these things in the name of Jesus, your son.
Amen.

(Adapted from *Rite of Acceptance into the Order of Catechumens*)

Sharing Our Good News

The leader invites members of the group to share how they lived the Good News since their last meeting.

Reflection 1

Baptized for holiness

In preparation for their infant son's Baptism, Brendan and Erin met with a catechist at their parish. The catechist led them through the Rite of Baptism, explaining what would happen in each part of the ceremony and the significance of each symbol of the rite. Periodically she paused to ask the couple various questions: Do you really "get" what you are accepting on behalf of your child? Do you realize what this means in terms of the way you live your faith? Do you know that when you are anointed with chrism as priest, prophet, and king that you are being commissioned to evangelize? Are you willing to accept your role in helping your son to live his faith, to share his faith, and to change the world because of his faith? Do you realize that the real work begins after receiving the sacrament of Baptism? Are you ready to be involved in mentoring your child in the faith and, in turn, open yourself to an ongoing and deeper relationship with Jesus Christ and the Church?

For Brendan, these questions hit him in a way that he did not expect. He felt walls crumbling within him and doors opening. He had never thought of Baptism in this way and wondered why no one had ever told him this before! He wondered how he had made it this far in life without ever making the connection that he had been commissioned, that he had been sent forth in baptism to build the reign of God here on earth. He realized that for the Church to be about its mission, he was going to have to make some decisions to be more intentional in sharing the gifts that God had given him.

Adapted from *Living Eucharist: Gathered, Nourished, Sent* (supplement), Bishop Robert Lynch

Eight Major Elements of the Liturgy of Baptism

"The meaning and grace of the sacrament of Baptism are clearly seen in the rites of its celebration" (*CCC*, 1234).

1. *The sign of the cross recalls Christ's saving death and the redemption it brought.*

2. *Readings from Scripture build the faith of all participants.*

3. *Exorcism and anointing call the person to be baptized to renounce sin.*

4. *Baptismal water is blessed so the person to be baptized may be 'born of water and the Spirit' (CCC, 1238).*

5. *Those being baptized renounce sin and profess faith.*

6. *Rite of Baptism: The bishop, priest or deacon either pours water three times on the person's head or immerses the candidate in water three times. The act is accompanied with the words, "[Name], I baptize you in the name of the Father, and of the Son, and of the Holy Spirit."*

7. *Anointing with Chrism: Sacred Chrism is a perfumed oil that signifies the gift of the Holy Spirit. The newly baptized is anointed so as to remain forever a member of Christ, who is Priest, Prophet and King.*

8. *The newly baptized is presented with a white garment, which shows the newly baptized has put on Christ and risen with him, and a candle, which is lit from the Paschal candle.*

Adapted from United States Catholic Catechism for Adults, pp.184-187

Baptism, Confirmation, and Eucharist are the three sacraments of initiation and "lay the foundations of every Christian life" (*CCC*, 1212). It is an important that they be understood together as a unifying whole. In Baptism, we are born anew and become sharers in the life of God. "By Baptism *all sins* are forgiven, original sin and all personal sins, as well as all punishment for sin (cf. Council of Florence [1439])" (*CCC*, 1263). The grace of Baptism enables us "to believe in God, to hope in him, and to love him", along with "the power to live and act under the prompting of the Holy Spirit", and the ability "to grow in goodness through the moral virtues" (*CCC*, 1266). In Baptism, we are called to share in Christ's Mission of proclaiming the Good News and furthering the reign of God here on earth. While this session focuses on Baptism, it is important to remember that Confirmation and the Eucharist are intrinsically connected to our Baptism. We "are strengthened by the sacrament of Confirmation, and we receive in the Eucharist the food of eternal life" (*CCC*, 1212).

Through Baptism, we are reborn into the Paschal Mystery—the life, death, and Resurrection of Jesus. In Baptism, we celebrate a new birth, a birth into the life of God. Jesus himself came to the Jordan to be baptized. John's use of water did not bring the gift of sharing God's life to God's only Son. Rather, Jesus' baptism was a sign of his solidarity with human beings in their need of divine forgiveness. Listen attentively to the story of Jesus' Baptism from Matthew.

Pondering the Word

Then Jesus came from Galilee

Matthew 3:13-17

Take a few minutes to savor a word, a phrase, a question, or a feeling that rises up in you. Reflect on this quietly or share it aloud.

Sharing Question

• At his Baptism, Jesus experienced the Spirit of God descending upon him and moving him to mission. How are you living as a disciple of Christ and steward of the gifts God has given you? Where are you on the path of living out your baptismal call and building the reign of God?

Reflection 2

Life-long conversion

The word Baptism is from the Greek *baptizein*, which means to "plunge" or "immerse." The waters of Baptism symbolize the plunge into Christ's death and Resurrection, enabling us to become "a new creature (2 Corinthians 5:17; Galatians 6:15; cf. Romans 6:3-4; Colossians 2:12)" (*CCC*, 1214). The newly baptized is not only freed from original sin and all personal sins but now shares in the hope of the Resurrection.

In the early Church, the bishop celebrated Baptism, Confirmation, and Eucharist together in one celebration during the Paschal Vigil. Through the centuries that practice changed due to the large number of converts and a developing theology of the meaning of each of these sacraments. It often became impossible for the bishop to be present to anoint and impose hands. Throughout the centuries, the age for the reception of Eucharist and Confirmation increased, so now in the Latin rite these sacraments are conferred at distinct times in our lives.

Today, when a child is baptized, the parents and godparents make the commitment to support that child in the growth of his or her faith. The entire community welcomes the child with the promise that it will strive to live the values of Jesus and incorporate the child into the life of the community, that is, the life of Jesus. "Baptism makes us members of the Body of Christ" (*CCC*, 1267). Baptism is the foundation of communion and community among all Christians, living and deceased. Through Baptism, we can truly say we are brothers and sisters in Jesus, called together to renew the face of the earth.

In the early Church, adults who wished to be baptized underwent a long period of preparation called the catechumenate. The word *catechumen* stems from both the Greek and Latin word meaning to *instruct*, and refers to a person receiving instruction and training in the Christian faith so he or she may be initiated into the Church. The early Church knew that the first sparks of faith in a convert have to be nurtured. This new Christian was formed in the catechumenate and confirmed by the sacraments of initiation. In this way, conversion would not only happen but find its way to maturity. This long period of the catechumenate included a series of preparatory rites, which were liturgical landmarks along the path of catechumenal preparation.

Following the Second Vatican Council, the order of the Catechumenate was restored in the Rite of Christian Initiation of Adults (RCIA). Today, the process begins with the precatechumenate, which is the initial period of inquiry and formation. The second stage is the catechumenate, which explores the teachings of the faith at a deeper level and in the context of prayer and worship. The third stage is purification and enlightenment, which coincides with Lent and is the period for catechumens to deepen their commitment. The culmination of these three stages is the Easter Vigil when the candidates are baptized, confirmed, and receive the Eucharist for the first time. They are officially welcomed into the community as full members. The final stage of the RCIA process is mystagogy, a period of post-baptismal catechesis when the community and the newly initiated deepen their understanding of the Paschal Mystery. They make it part of their lives through meditation on the Gospel, sharing in the Eucharist, announcing the Good News, and performing works of charity and justice.

As Church, it is our fundamental task and responsibility to welcome new members into a caring community of faith. Through the catechumenate, we are invited to instruct them in the richness of our faith, accompanying them on their journey with prayer, witness and good example. Within the rite itself, we experience a model of Church that is communal. The entire Christian community is called to provide welcome and hospitality, and each of us is called to share our personal faith in Jesus, to evangelize, to catechize, and to enter more deeply into the Paschal Mystery of Jesus.

Sharing Our Faith

- What have I done to continue the conversion process started at my Baptism? If I were baptized as an adult, what led me to this choice?

- If I have asked for Baptism for my child or children, why? How did this experience influence my life/my faith? If my spouse, a family member or friend asked for Baptism as an adult, did this experience challenge me? If so, how?

- How do I experience the Christian initiation process in my parish?

- In what ways does our parish welcome the newly baptized? If we have not done so, how might our parish welcome them in some concrete way?

Living the Good News

Determine a specific action (individual or group) that flows from your sharing. This should be your primary consideration for choosing an action.

If choosing an individual action, determine what you will do and share it with the group. If choosing a group action, determine who will take responsibility for different aspects of the action.

The following are secondary suggestions:

- Take part in the Easter Vigil this year, paying particular attention to the renewal of baptismal vows. Pray over the vows during the week.

Original Sin

"By Baptism all sins are forgiven, Original Sin and all personal sins, and temporal punishment due to sin is removed. After one has been reborn in Christ, there is nothing to prevent one's entry into God's Kingdom.

However, though all sins are removed, there remains, as an effect of Original Sin, the inclination to sin that is called *concupiscence*. This inclination to sin shows itself in what is sometimes referred to as a darkening of the mind and a weakening of the will, that is, the inability to know clearly the right or wrong of an action and/or the lack of strength to resist temptation and always to do the right thing no matter how hard this is. The effects of Original Sin need not harm us so long as we seek strength to resist them through the Sacrament of Penance, the Sacrament of the Eucharist, prayer, a deepening spirituality, growth in virtue, and a wholehearted dependence on God."

United States Catholic Catechism for Adults, p.192

- Talk with your parents or godparents and ask them to recall your baptismal day, or share with your child or godchild what his or her baptism meant for you.

- Make a commitment to become a regular part of a small Christian community or seasonal small community in your parish. If your parish does not have small communities, talk with your pastor and pastoral staff about the possibility of initiating them.

- Organize the parents of newly baptized or soon-to-be-baptized children into a small group for reflection and faith sharing around the sacrament. RENEW International offers *Preparing for Your Child's Baptism,* a six-week faith-sharing book. For more information, visit **www.renewintl.org/store.**

In light of this session, this week I commit to:

_____

_____

Lifting Our Hearts

Leader	In Baptism, we celebrate a new birth into the life of God. Jesus himself came to the Jordan to be baptized as a sign of his solidarity with us human beings in our need for divine forgiveness.
	Let us begin our prayer by saying "Yes" to God in the renewal of our baptismal promises.
	Pause, until each member has a lighted candle.
Leader	Do you reaffirm your renunciation of evil and renew your commitment to Jesus Christ?
All	**I do.**
Leader	Do you believe in God the Father?
All	**I believe in God, the Father almighty, creator of heaven and earth.**
Leader	Do you believe in Jesus Christ, the Son of God?
All	**I believe in Jesus Christ, his only Son, our Lord.**
	He was conceived by the power of the Holy Spirit and born of the Virgin Mary.

	He suffered under Pontius Pilate, was crucified, died and was buried.
	He ascended into heaven, and is seated at the right hand of the Father.
	He will come again to judge the living and the dead.
Leader	Do you believe in the Holy Spirit?
All	**I believe in the Holy Spirit, the holy catholic Church, the communion of saints, the forgiveness of sins, the resurrection of the body, and the life everlasting.**
Leader	May Almighty God, the Father of Our Lord Jesus Christ, who has given us a new birth by water and the Holy Spirit, and bestowed upon us the forgiveness of sins, keep us in eternal life by his grace, in Christ Jesus our Lord.
All	**Amen.**

Looking Ahead

- Prepare for your next session by prayerfully reading and studying:
  - Session 5: Confirmation: Sealed With the Spirit;
  - Scripture: Galatians 5:16-17, 22-26;
  - Chapter 16, pages 201-211, "Confirmation: Consecrated for Mission" in the *United States Catholic Catechism for Adults;*
  - paragraphs 1285-1321 of the *Catechism of the Catholic Church.*
- Remember to use RENEWING FAMILY FAITH and its helpful suggestions on how to extend the fruits of your sharing beyond your group, especially to your families (see pages 96-97).

SESSION FIVE

Confirmation:
Sealed with the Spirit

Suggested Environment

Bible, candle, and a small table on which a Bible may be enthroned. Consider decorating the table with colors of the liturgical year and symbols of Confirmation such as chrism or oil, a photo of the laying on of hands from a Confirmation ceremony, etc.

In addition it is suggested that the Catechism of the Catholic Church (CCC) *and the* United States Catholic Catechism for Adults (USCCA) *be available.*

Begin with a quiet, reflective atmosphere.

Lifting Our Hearts

Song Suggestion

"Send Us Your Spirit," David Haas (GIA)

Prayer

Pray together

Come, Holy Spirit, fill our hearts with your holy gifts.

(Prayed alternately by two people or two groups)

Side 1	Let our weakness be penetrated with your strength this very day that we may do what is right and just.
Side 2	Let our love and charity be such as to offend no one, and hurt no one's feelings, so generous as to pardon any wrongs done to us.
All	**Come, Holy Spirit, fill our hearts with your holy gifts.**
Side 1	Assist us, O Holy Spirit, in all the trials of life; enlighten us in our uncertainty; advise us in our

doubts; strengthen us in our weakness; help us in all our
needs; protect us in times of temptation;
and console us in affliction.

Side 2   Assist us to live holy lives
and to grow in goodness and grace.
Graciously hear us, O Holy Spirit, and pour your light
into our bodies, hearts, minds, and souls.

All   **Come, Holy Spirit, fill our hearts with your holy gifts.
Amen.**

Sharing Our Good News

*The leader invites members of the group to share how they lived the Good
News since their last meeting.*

Reflection 1

Gift of the Holy Spirit

It had been many years since Sofia received the sacrament of
Confirmation, and she rarely thought about the experience. One
summer, a colleague at work, Betsy, invited her to join a group of
young adults who were renting a beach house. Betsy and the other
people in the house were members of an independent Christian
church. They described themselves as "born again," and they were
friendly and welcomed Sofia into their group. Although she did not
feel she truly belonged, she was impressed with the way they lived
their faith. They all chipped in to buy groceries to prepare dinner,
which they ate together. They also prayed before meals, and she
would notice some of them reading the Bible in the quiet hours of the
morning. While barrels of empty beer cans and liquor bottles collected
in front of other beach houses, Sofia's new housemates did not drink
alcohol or go to bars. One day while hanging out on the beach, some
of her housemates began taking swipes at the Catholic Church.
Instinctively, Sofia began defending the faith of her childhood. One of
the "born-again" Christians became confrontational with her, asking,
"What do you believe?" She was uncomfortable with being put on the
spot, but she silently prayed to the Holy Spirit for guidance. With new
assurance she began answering their questions while at the same time
realizing how much her faith was a part of her.

Confirmation, like Baptism and Eucharist, is a sacrament of initiation. Confirmation reaffirms what God has already given us in Baptism, deepens our baptismal life, and strengthens our relationship with Christ. "[T]he reception of the sacrament of Confirmation is necessary for the completion of baptismal grace (cf. *Roman Ritual*, Rite of Confirmation [OC], Introduction 1)" (*CCC*, 1285). In Confirmation, we celebrate that God loves us and is with us. God promises again to be with us always and fulfills that promise by the living presence of the Holy Spirit within us through the sacrament of Confirmation. At the moment when Sofia needed the graces of Confirmation, the Spirit was with her to answer her friends' questions and to affirm her in her faith.

Over and over in the Old Testament, the prophets proclaimed that the Spirit of God would be upon the Messiah. In the Gospels, we read that Jesus was conceived of the Holy Spirit (Luke 1:35), and that Spirit guided and enlightened Jesus along every step of his journey (*CCC*, 1286). When Jesus, the Messiah, came to the Jordan to be baptized by John, the Holy Spirit overshadowed him (Matthew 3:16-17, Mark 1:9-11, Luke 3:21-22). At the Last Supper, Jesus promised to send the Spirit, the Advocate, to his disciples to teach them all things (John 14:26). After his resurrection, Jesus breathed the Holy Spirit upon them (John 20:22-23). At the moment of Pentecost, the disciples were filled with the Holy Spirit and began to proclaim the "mighty works of God" (Acts 2:11) (*CCC*, 1287). We, too, are promised the same Spirit.

Spotlight on the *Catechism*

"In continuity with the New Testament custom of laying hands on those who would receive the gift of the Spirit, the bishop extends his two hands over all those to be confirmed. He recites a prayer that begs the Father of our Lord Jesus Christ for the outpouring of the Holy Spirit and for the seven gifts traditionally associated with the Spirit. These gifts are permanent dispositions that move us to respond to the guidance of the Spirit. The traditional list of the gifts is based on Isaiah 11:1-3: wisdom, understanding, knowledge, counsel, fortitude, piety (reverence), and fear of the Lord (wonder and awe in God's presence)."

United States Catholic Catechism for Adults, p. 205

Pondering the Word

The fruit of the spirit is love

Galatians 5:16-17, 22-26

Take a few minutes to savor a word, a phrase, a question, or a feeling that rises up in you. Reflect on this quietly or share it aloud.

Sharing Question

- According to the Scripture reading, the fruits of the Holy Spirit are love, joy, peace, patience, kindness, generosity, faithfulness, gentleness, and self-control. Which spiritual fruits are ripening in me? Which still need more time and warmth of God's love to develop?

Reflection 2

Empowered by the Spirit

The scriptural account that most closely parallels the gift of the Spirit in the sacrament of Confirmation is the Pentecost event (Acts of the Apostles 2:1-4). The presence of the Spirit comes with the sound of rushing wind and the appearance of tongues of fire over each disciple's head. The promise of Jesus is fulfilled and a fearful group of disciples is emboldened to preach with the power of the Holy Spirit. Their transformation as proclaimers of God's mighty deeds resulted in the Baptism of thousands on that day, and a lifetime of fruitful proclamation of the Good News.

The action of laying on of hands is an ancient practice that signifies the conferring of power by one person to another. Moses lays his hands on Joshua to make him his successor (Numbers 27:15-23), and Isaac lays his hand on his son Jacob to transfer authority over the tribe (Genesis 27:18-29). In the Catholic tradition, the laying on of hands is recognized as the origin of the Sacrament of Confirmation.

In the Old Testament, anointing with oil was used to commission kings and priests. Jesus, the Christ (meaning "anointed one"), is Priest, Prophet and King. By the second century, anointing with blessed oil was included in the ritual for the celebration of Confirmation. In the words of Pope Paul VI, "the sacrament of Confirmation is conferred through the anointing with chrism on the forehead, which is done by the laying on of the hand, and through the words: "Be sealed with the gift of the Holy Spirit" (*Divinae consortium naturae*, 663).

Through the anointing of Confirmation, the Christian is marked permanently with the seal of the Holy Spirit signifying our total belonging to Christ. "A seal is a symbol of a person, a sign of personal authority, or ownership of an object (cf. Genesis 38:18; 41:42;

Deuteronomy 32:34; *Catechesi tradendae* 8:6)" (*CCC*, 1295). "This seal of the Holy Spirit marks our total belonging to Christ" (*CCC*, 1296).

Sacred chrism, used in the sacrament of Confirmation is consecrated by the bishop for the diocese at the Chrism Mass during Holy Week. Sacred Chrism is also used in Baptism to anoint infants and in Ordination to anoint priests and bishops. The bishop is the ordinary minister of Confirmation (*CCC*, 1313). Bishops signify both the local and diocesan Church and emphasize our communion in the universal Church. Confirmation confirms us in our mission to the whole world. We are called and empowered to help renew the face of the earth: to bring love, justice and peace to all, especially those devoid of love.

Through the outpouring of the Holy Spirit at Confirmation, we become more aware that God is with us and within us. The power of the sacrament unites us more closely with Jesus and confirms our baptismal call to share in his mission. At Confirmation we receive the gifts of the Holy Spirit, who empowers and strengthens us to bring the Good News of Jesus to the world. Through Confirmation, we are strengthened to live our faith in the ordinary and extraordinary circumstances of our lives. Whether we are at work, in our homes, or in the social or political arena, we can make choices based on gospel values. Like the disciples at Pentecost, we go forth to love

Effects of Confirmation

It is evident from its celebration that the effect of the sacrament of Confirmation is the special outpouring of the Holy Spirit as once granted to the apostles on the day of Pentecost.

From this fact, Confirmation brings an increase and deepening of baptismal grace:

- *It roots us more deeply in the divine filiation which makes us cry, "Abba! Father!" (Romans 8:15);*
- *It unites us more firmly to Christ;*
- *It increases the gifts of the Holy Spirit in us;*
- *It renders our bond with the Church more perfect (cf.* Lumen gentium, *11);*
- *It gives us a special strength of the Holy Spirit to spread and defend the faith by word and action as true witnesses of Christ, to confess the name of Christ boldly, and never to be ashamed of the Cross (cf. Council of Florence [1439];* Lumen gentium, *11,12):*

Recall then that you have received the spiritual seal, the spirit of wisdom and understanding, the spirit of right judgment and courage, the spirit of knowledge and reverence, the spirit of holy fear in God's presence. Guard what you have received. God the Father has marked you with his sign; Christ the Lord has confirmed you and has placed his pledge, the Spirit, in your hearts (St. Ambrose, *De myst.* 7, 42).

Catechism of the Catholic Church, 1302-1303

and serve God and one another. We need no longer be shy or timid; rather, we are full of the strength of God (*CCC*, 1303).

The reality of Pentecost is present in a special manner in the celebration of the sacrament of Confirmation as we receive the gifts of the Holy Spirit. Just as the apostles called upon the gift received at Pentecost throughout their lives, so too, the grace of Confirmation remains present in us by our active commitment to the Christian life. To fully avail of the grace of Confirmation, we deepen our faith relationship with God through the celebration of the sacraments, prayer, Scripture reading, study of our faith, and through our conscious decisions to do God's will and to follow Christ day by day.

Sharing Our Faith

- The symbols and actions of Confirmation are wind, fire, oil, anointing, and laying on of hands. What do the symbols of Confirmation mean to me?

- The Holy Spirit bestows seven gifts: wisdom, understanding, knowledge, fortitude, counsel, piety, and fear of the Lord. What are the gifts of the Holy Spirit that I am aware of in my life?

- When in my life have I experienced the power of the Spirit in helping me witness to Christ in my words or deeds?

- How can I respond to the outpouring of the Holy Spirit in my life today?

Living the Good News

Determine a specific action (individual or group) that flows from your sharing. This should be your primary consideration for choosing an action.

If choosing an individual action, determine what you will do and share it with the group. If choosing a group action, determine who will take responsibility for different aspects of the action.

The following are secondary suggestions:

- Offer to assist in the preparation of those celebrating the sacrament of Confirmation in your parish.

- Choose an area in the world that is desperately in need of healing, love, justice, and peace. Offer assistance in a way that is possible for you, through prayer, donation, or volunteering.

- Volunteer this week to help address injustice in your community. Contact your diocesan or parish social justice office or the county volunteer office for a schedule of upcoming activities.

Pray for this week In light of this session, this week I commit to:

Rita Jenny Dough Audry Jim Sharon Mike ?? Wilson

Lifting Our Hearts

Offer prayers of thanks for all the gifts of the Holy Spirit you have received.

Pray together

God our Father,
complete the work you have begun
and keep the gifts of your Holy Spirit
active in the hearts of your people.

Make them ready to live his Gospel
and eager to do his will.

May they never be ashamed
to proclaim to all the world Christ crucified
living and reigning for ever and ever. Amen

(From the Rite of Confirmation, 33)

Looking Ahead

- Prepare for your next session by prayerfully reading and studying:
  - Session 6: Eucharist: The Real Presence of Christ;
  - Scripture: John 6:48-58;
  - Chapter 17, pages 201-211, "The Eucharist: Source and Summit of the Christian Life" in the *United States Catholic Catechism for Adults;*
  - paragraphs 1322-1419 of the *Catechism of the Catholic Church.*
- Remember to use RENEWING FAMILY FAITH and its helpful suggestions on how to extend the fruits of your sharing beyond your group, especially to your families (see pages 96-97).

Eucharist:
The Real Presence of Christ

Suggested Environment

Bible, candle, and a small table on which a Bible may be enthroned. Consider decorating the table with colors of the liturgical year and symbols of the Eucharist such as bread and wine.

In addition it is suggested that the Catechism of the Catholic Church (CCC) *and the* United States Catholic Catechism for Adults (USCCA) *be available.*

Begin with a quiet, reflective atmosphere.

Lifting Our Hearts

Song Suggestion

"Eat This Bread," Robert Batastini, Taizé, and Jacques Berthier (GIA)

Prayer

Pray together

God, our Father, Creator of the universe,
You gave us Jesus who transformed simple bread and wine
into his body and blood.

As we gather to reflect upon this great gift of the Eucharist,
open our hearts to your Word
and to the power of your Holy Spirit in our lives today.
Help us to share our lives with others as Jesus shares life with us.
Open our hearts to the hungry in this world,
so we will always feed one another.

Help us always to receive the risen Jesus with love and praise
and to receive one another with peace and harmony.
We ask this through Jesus.
Amen.

"They devoted themselves to the apostles' teaching and fellowship, to the breaking of bread and the prayers.... Day by day, as they spent much time together in the temple, they broke bread at home and ate their food with glad and generous hearts, praising God and having the goodwill of all the people. And day by day the Lord added to their number those who were being saved."

Acts of the Apostles 2:42, 46-47

Sharing Our Good News

The leader invites members of the group to share how they lived the Good News since their last meeting.

Reflection 1

Sacrament of thanksgiving

Jack began coming to Sunday Eucharist every week. He always seemed sad and didn't mix with the others in the small community. As I got to know him, I learned that he was unemployed and felt little hope to get a job. I also noticed that he did not come forward to receive Communion; he remained in the pew, head down, praying intensely. One day after Mass, Jack told me he was recently divorced and had relocated to our area seeking employment.

"The worst part of this whole mess is that I can't receive Communion any more because now I'm excommunicated by the divorce." Knowing that he was not remarried, I explained that he could receive Communion. At first he looked at me in disbelief. I nodded my head. A faint smile began to light up his face. "You mean I can receive the sacraments? That's a fact?"

"Yes, you can, Jack," I assured him, and he grinned broadly.

The following Sunday, Jack came in looking happier than I'd ever seen him. As he approached me to receive Communion, his face was aglow with joy. After Mass, he told me, "I'm just so grateful, so grateful to Jesus for coming to me! I missed Communion so much, and I thought I was condemned forever to be deprived of the sacraments. I spent all of Mass thanking God, even for the hard times, and I feel new strength now to deal with my problems. Thanks so much for your help."

On the night before he died, Jesus gathered his disciples together for the Passover meal, a ritual Thanksgiving meal remembering and celebrating the saving actions of God who brought the Israelites out of Egypt. On this night, Jesus added something new to the ritual. Giving thanks to God, Jesus blessed, broke and shared the bread, his body, and passed the cup of wine, his blood, instructing his disciples to, "Do this in memory of me." At that Last Supper, Jesus "instituted the Eucharist as the memorial of his death and Resurrection" (*CCC*, 1337).

Bread and wine have long been a source of sustenance to humanity. They are signs of God's generosity through the goodness of the earth and the work of human hands. Both have held special meaning in our salvation history. On the night beginning their Exodus from Egypt, the Israelites ate unleavened bread, signifying the urgency of their escape. In the desert, they ate manna, a bread-like substance sent from God to sustain them for their journey. The Jewish people continue even today to eat unleavened bread for their celebration of Passover, recalling God's saving actions and faithfulness past and present. The cup of wine in the Jewish Passover celebrates the expectation of the one who is to come to save Israel. Jesus used these very symbols to fulfill his promises to be with us always and to give us food for our journey (*CCC*, 1334). No wonder that Jack, in the story above, mistakenly felt so disappointed at being deprived of Holy Communion, the food for his journey. Once he received Communion, he felt that he had the divine help to face all the problems of his life.

After the Pentecost experience, as the fledgling Church strove to live life as Jesus had modeled for them, the disciples continued to gather as a community of faith by meeting in homes for prayer, to read Scriptures, and for the "breaking of the bread." These celebrations, where bread was blessed in thanksgiving, broken, and shared was a means of entering again the life, death and resurrection of Jesus, were known as Eucharist, from the word *eucharistia*, which means "thanksgiving."

Adults who are initiated into the Catholic Church receive Baptism, Confirmation, and then Eucharist. Eucharist completes Christian initiation (*CCC*, 1322). The usual custom for those baptized as infants in the Latin Rite is to receive Eucharist before Confirmation.

Listen attentively as Jesus describes himself as the Bread of Life.

Spotlight on the *Catechism*

"Since the Middle Ages, the change of bread and wine into the Body and Blood of Christ has been called 'transubstantiation.' This means that the substance of the bread and wine is changed into the substance of the body and Blood of Christ. The appearances of bread and wine remain (color, shape, weight, chemical composition), but the underlying reality—that is, the substance—is now the Body and Blood of Christ."

United States Catholic Catechism for Adults, p. 223

Pondering the Word

'I am the Bread of Life'

John 6:48-58

Take a few minutes to savor a word, a phrase, a question, or a feeling that rises up in you. Reflect on this quietly or share it aloud.

Sharing Question

- Do I come to the Eucharist expecting to be fed or do I sometimes look for other ways to feed my hungers?

Reflection 2

Sacrament of presence

For nearly 2,000 years, Catholics have responded to Jesus' command to "do this in memory of me" every time we celebrate Mass. In this "memorial" Jesus becomes fully and truly present with us. We experience his presence even as we gather for the Mass for "where two or three are gathered in my name, I am in their midst" (Matthew 18:20).

The Eucharistic celebration starts with the Introductory Rites, a call to prayer that begins with the sign of the Cross. Thus we affirm our faith as Trinitarian and our belief that we are called to that same communion of love as the Father, Son, and Holy Spirit. In the Penitential Rite, we ask forgiveness for our failures to live in communion with God and with one another.

In the Liturgy of the Word (Scripture readings, homily, and the prayer of the faithful) we are nourished as well as challenged to live according to God's ways. Then, the bread and wine are brought to the altar where "they will be offered by the priest in the name of Christ in the Eucharistic sacrifice in which they will become his body and blood" (*CCC*, 1350).

The Eucharistic Prayer recalls the events of Jesus' Paschal Mystery, making present the saving action of God through Christ. This remembering, or memorial, is called anamnesis. When we celebrate Eucharist, we celebrate Christ's Passover, not only as a memorial of some past event, but also as an event that is real and present to us today (*CCC*, 1364). Anamnesis is the act of recalling, of calling to mind, of making present, of actualizing. The church recalls or makes an anamnesis of what the Father has completed through Christ in human salvation. Through anamnesis, God's marvelous deeds are recalled by the liturgical assembly and are made present in their midst.

When the Church makes memory, it is accompanied by epiclesis, the invocation of the Holy Spirit who will consecrate or "make holy" the people and the sacramental elements. Epiclesis is an invocation of the Holy Spirit upon the people and the sacramental elements. "In the epiclesis, the Church asks the Father to send his Holy Spirit…on the bread and wine, so that by his power they may become the body and blood of Jesus Christ and so that those who take part in the Eucharist may be one body and one spirit" (CCC, 1353). Epiclesis completes and culminates the action of anamnesis. Anamnesis leads to epiclesis just as the Paschal Mystery led to Pentecost. In liturgy we not only recall the Paschal Mystery, we also receive the Holy Spirit.

During the consecration, the celebrant recites with great reverence the words of Jesus, instituting the Holy Eucharist, after which the assembly proclaims the great mystery of our faith: the Paschal Mystery made present in the Eucharistic celebration. The Eucharistic Prayer then continues with the intercessions including invocations that we make with Mary and the saints. The Eucharistic Prayer closes with the great doxology, "Through Him, with Him and in Him …" to which we respond "Amen." St. Jerome taught that our Amen should resound like a giant thunderclap, affirming our assent to what has been said and done in the name of the people.

We begin our immediate preparation for the reception of the Eucharist by praying the Our Father and exchanging a sign of peace. As the celebrant breaks the Body of Christ, or fraction, the people interpret what they are seeing by singing the Lamb of God. We are then invited to the table of the Lord to receive Communion. We approach with the faith of the centurion who said, "Lord, I am not worthy to have you come under my roof; but only speak the word, and my servant will be healed" (Matthew 8:8).

In the Concluding Rites, the priest calls down upon us the final blessing of the celebration. We make the sign of the cross (as we did at the beginning of Mass) and are dismissed to become bread for the world. The word "Mass" stems from the ancient Latin dismissal, *Ite, missa est,* for which the literal translation is "Go, it is sent." In the context of the liturgy, this means "what we have come here together to do is done, now go out and fulfill it."

The Church invites us to take part in the Eucharist in a full, active, and conscious way. This means that we bring ourselves as we

Sacrament of Charity

"The sacrament of charity, the Holy Eucharist is the gift that Jesus Christ makes of himself, thus revealing to us God's infinite love for every man and woman. This wondrous sacrament makes manifest that 'greater' love which led him to 'lay down his life for his friends' (John 15:13). Jesus did indeed love them 'to the end' (John 13:1). In those words the Evangelist introduces Christ's act of immense humility: before dying for us on the Cross, he tied a towel around himself and washed the feet of his disciples. In the same way, Jesus continues, in the sacrament of the Eucharist, to love us 'to the end,' even to offering us his body and his blood. What amazement must the Apostles have felt in witnessing what the Lord did and said during that Supper! What wonder must the eucharistic mystery also awaken in our own hearts!"

Pope Benedict XVI, *Sacramentum Caritatis*, 1

are to the sacred altar and surrender ourselves to the Lord who will transform us into his better disciples through the Eucharistic celebration. At the heart of every Eucharistic celebration are the bread and wine that, when consecrated, become Christ's Body and Blood. In each form of the Eucharist Christ is fully present "by the power of the Holy Spirit through the ministry of the priest's acting in the person of Christ during the Eucharistic Prayer" (*USCCA*, p. 229). It is this real presence, Jesus himself, that we receive and carry with us in Holy Communion. Hence receiving Holy Communion is a natural part of full and active participation in the Eucharistic celebration.

When we receive the body and blood of Christ, we become one with him. St. Augustine taught, "You are the body of Christ and his members. You reply, 'Amen' to that which you are, and by replying you consent. For you hear 'The body of Christ,' and you reply 'Amen.' Be a member of the body of Christ so that your 'Amen' may be true. Be what you see, and receive what you are" (Sermon 272). Through the Eucharist we share in the very life, death, and resurrection of Christ and become the Christian community, the Church, the presence of Jesus Christ in the world.

Our Catholic tradition says the Church makes the Eucharist, and the Eucharist makes the Church. As members of the Church, we cannot achieve this transformation through our own efforts. "Only Jesus can transform us into himself. Our inner receptivity is critical. To receive love, we need to be open to it. The sacrificial gift of self at every Mass is the best way to be continuously transformed into Christ. Then in Christ we become bread for the world's bodily and spiritual hungers" (*USCCA*, p. 227).

The "body of Christ" we receive from the altar implies reaching out and embracing the larger "body of Christ" consisting of our brothers and sisters out there—in need of our attention, understanding and concern. Christ then becomes present and visible in and through us. We become sacraments to others. The living and transforming experience of the Mass extends even beyond what we do around the altar in church.

Sharing Our Faith

- In everyday life, what do bread and wine symbolize for me?
- In what ways does the Eucharist, the bread of life, create life in me?
- What new insights have I had into the Eucharistic Prayer as my prayer?
- How am I transformed to be bread for the world? What holds me back from being bread for others?

Living the Good News

Determine a specific action (individual or group) that flows from your sharing. This should be your primary consideration for choosing an action.

If choosing an individual action, determine what you will do and share it with the group. If choosing a group action, determine who will take responsibility for different aspects of the action.

The following are secondary suggestions:

- When you participate in the Eucharistic liturgy, consider what it means to present the bread and wine as gifts, to give thanks, to be bread that is broken. Journal your insights and consider how you might respond to a fuller understanding of communion.
- Check with your diocesan Office of Worship or Liturgy for upcoming catechetical formation programs on Eucharist or liturgy. Participate in one, if circumstances allow.
- As Christians we receive spiritual nourishment through the Body and Blood of Christ in the Eucharist. Prayerfully consider joining a parish ministry that will allow you to supply the daily bread people need for physical nourishment.

In light of this session, this week I commit to:

_____

_____

Lifting Our Hearts

Offer spontaneous prayers of thanksgiving to God and conclude by praying the following together:

You so loved the world, Father most holy,
that in the fullness of time
you sent your Only Begotten Son to be our Savior.

Incarnate by the Holy Spirit and born of the Virgin Mary,
he shared our human nature in all things but sin.

To the poor he proclaimed the good news of salvation,
to prisoners, freedom, and to the sorrowful of heart, joy.

To accomplish your plan, he have himself up to death,
and rising, from the dead, he destroyed death and restored life.

And that we might live no longer for ourselves
but for him who died and rose again for us,
he sent the Holy Spirit from you, Father,
as the first fruits for those who believe,
so that bringing to perfection his work in the world,
he might sanctify creation to the full. Amen.

(*Adapted from* Eucharistic Prayer IV)

Looking Ahead

- Prepare for your next session by prayerfully reading and studying:
  - Session 7: Penance and Reconciliation: God Rich in Mercy;
  - Scripture: Luke 15:11-32;
  - Chapter 18, pages 234-247, "Sacrament of Penance and Reconciliation: God is Rich in Mercy" in the *United States Catholic Catechism for Adults;*
  - paragraphs 1420-1498 of the *Catechism of the Catholic Church.*
- Remember to use RENEWING FAMILY FAITH and its helpful suggestions on how to extend the fruits of your sharing beyond your group, especially to your families (see pages 96-97).

Penance and Reconciliation: God Rich in Mercy

Suggested Environment

Bible, candle, and a small table on which a Bible may be enthroned. Consider decorating the table with colors of the liturgical year and other symbols of Penance and Reconciliation such as a stole and an image of the return of the prodigal son.

In addition it is suggested that the Catechism of the Catholic Church (CCC) *and the* United States Catholic Catechism for Adults (USCCA) *be available.*

Begin with a quiet, reflective atmosphere.

Lifting Our Hearts

Song Suggestion

"Hosea," Gregory Norbet (Weston Priory)

Prayer

Pray together

Open our eyes to see the evil we have done.
Touch our hearts and convert us to yourself.

Where sin has divided and scattered,
may your love make one again;
Where sin has brought weakness,
may your power heal and strengthen;
where sin has brought death,
may your Spirit raise to new life.

Give us a new heart to love you,
so that our lives may reflect the image of your Son.

May the world see the glory of Christ
revealed in your Church,
and come to know

that he is the one whom you have sent,
Jesus Christ, your Son, our Lord.
Amen.

(Rite of Penance, 99)

Sharing Our Good News

The leader invites members of the group to share how they lived the Good News since their last meeting.

Reflection 1

The good shepherd

In November 1993, Cardinal Joseph Bernardin, archbishop of Chicago, was accused of sexually abusing a former seminarian. The young man, Steven Cook, in his mid-thirties and very ill with AIDS, had been a seminarian at St. Gregory's Seminary in Cincinnati, where the cardinal had served as archbishop at the time. As news of the accusation spread throughout the world, the cardinal felt deep humiliation. Believing that the truth would prevail, the cardinal denied the charges in statements and at press conferences. He soon came to believe that Steven, who had previously accused a priest on the seminary's faculty of sexually abusing him, had been manipulated by his lawyer into making the new accusation against him. Eventually Steven asked the judge in federal court to drop the charges.

As Cardinal Bernardin learned more about Steven's life, he began to see him as the sheep that had been lost and that he should follow his shepherd's calling to seek him out. He felt the experience of the false accusation would not be complete until he met and reconciled with Steven. They met in December 1994, and Steven admitted that Cardinal Bernardin had not abused him. He apologized for the hurt and embarrassment he had caused. The cardinal accepted his apology and asked if he would like him to celebrate Mass for him. At first Steven was unsure. He had been deeply alienated from God and the Church for a long time. The cardinal gave him a Bible he had inscribed for him, and Steven pressed the Bible to his heart as tears welled up in his eyes. Then the cardinal gave him a chalice that had been given to him to say Mass for Steven some day. "Please," Steven responded tearfully, "let's celebrate Mass now." During the Mass, they embraced in the sign of peace, and afterwards the cardinal anointed

Steven with the sacrament of the sick. He said that in his entire priesthood he had never witnessed a more profound reconciliation.

Adapted from *The Gift of Peace: Personal Reflections by Joseph Cardinal Bernardin*

Cardinal Bernardin's actions toward Steven Cook echo Scripture's portrayal of a God who invites us to surrender our fears to his generous love and live a new life through his grace. Knowing that his accuser must have been in terrible emotional pain, and also concerned about the young man's health, the cardinal reached out to him seeking reconciliation. He did not desire retribution for the ordeal of being falsely accused of sexual abuse. All he wanted was an acknowledgement of the truth and sincere contrition. Likewise, Steven wanted to tell the truth and ask forgiveness. In response, the cardinal gave him gifts and celebrated Mass for him and the sacrament of Anointing of the Sick. Cardinal Bernardin, like God, was "rich in mercy."

To fully appreciate the sacrament of Penance and Reconciliation today, we must first understand that from the beginning of time God desired to reconcile all of creation to himself. The prophets called the people to repentance and reconciliation. Jesus' own life, suffering, death, and resurrection was a supreme act of reconciliation. As St. Paul writes so encouragingly to the community at Corinth: "So whoever is in Christ is a new creation: the old things have passed away; behold, new things have come. And all this is from God, who has reconciled us to himself through Christ and given us the ministry of reconciliation; namely, God was reconciling the world to himself in Christ, not counting their trespasses against them and entrusting to us the message of reconciliation" (2 Corinthians 5:17-19).

The sacrament of conversion, of turning away from sin and toward God, in the New Testament is Baptism. But what we are made by God in Baptism then has to be lived out. "Conversion" is life long, the standard way of Christian life. The Gospel tells us the basic ways to express this fundamental attitude are through prayer, fasting, almsgiving, and other good works (Matthew 6:1-18).

However, it is also clear in the New Testament that there were some sinful actions that clearly demonstrate, in a public way, that the individual has abandoned his or her baptismal promises. Examples were apostasy (denying the faith), murder, and adultery. In such cases, what was needed was a major "re-conversion." This re-conversion was modeled on the first sacrament of conversion, namely Baptism.

What are the different forms of the Sacrament of Penance?

The Sacrament of Penance takes three forms. Pope Paul VI's eloquent explanation of each rite is provided below (Pope Paul VI, General Audience [April 3, 1974]).

1. The Rite for the Reconciliation of Individual Penitents

"The first [form] is the reconciliation of an individual . . . with a new emphasis on the demand for personal dispositions and on the relationship to the word of God. . . . This form of reconciliation is the accustomed one, but enriched by a greater awareness, seriousness, listening, and so to speak, by a new outpouring of divine love and our own inexpressible joy in the knowledge of being restored to divine life. . . ."

2. The Rite for the Reconciliation of Several Penitents

"The second way of reconciliation is that of a communal preparation followed by individual confession and absolution. It combines the two values of being a community act and a personal act. It is a preferable form of reconciliation for our people when it is possible but it usually presupposes the presence of many ministers of the sacrament and this is not always easy."

3. The Rite for the Reconciliation of Several Penitents with General Absolution

"Then there is the third way, a collective form of reconciliation with a single, general absolution. This form, however, is by way of exception, of necessity, in cases sanctioned by the bishops, and with the continuing obligation of individual [confession] of grave sins, that is, mortal sins, at a later time."

United States Conference of Catholic Bishops, *Celebrating the Sacrament of Penance: Questions and Answers*

In the same way catechumens went through a rite of entry, so did "penitents." Like the catechumenate, it lasted several years, long enough for the penitents to prove themselves. The ashes that mark our foreheads at the beginning of Lent can be traced to part of this ancient ceremony. When the community judged they were ready, the penitents were reconciled at a Mass on Holy Thursday morning, presided by the bishop (so that they would be ready to take full part in the Church's greatest feast, the Paschal Vigil).

The oldest references we have to the sacrament outside of the New Testament speak of "second baptism." Ambrose, for example, talks of the two conversions, one by water, the other by tears (Letter 41:12). Just as Baptism could be received only once, so, too, the Church ruled, Penance could be received only once. The severity of the process and the fact it could only be celebrated once had two unintended consequences: people postponed it to as late as possible in life, and it became widespread to wait until the deathbed.

As time went on, a private form of penance developed. The Celtic church was built on a pattern of communities centered around monasteries rather than parishes, and where most of the monks were ordained priests. As in all monastic traditions, many monks acted as spiritual advisors offering counsel on Christian life in general, and in particular how to reshape whatever was wrong in one's life. From the sixth century onward, the sinner came to the monk/priest seeking God's forgiveness, which was expressed through absolution.

The missionary Celtic monks brought this tradition with them into Europe. Some local churches resisted this practice; others adopted it. The positive value of the personal spiritual guidance in this practice plus the assurance of forgiveness for "private" sins obviously corresponded to a pastoral need, and by the Middle Ages this practice was commonplace. The two practices were complementary, existing in parallel: "public" penance for public sins, a "private" form for private sins.

The Scholastic reflection (12th century) on the sacraments, now definitively recognized as seven, explored how each had "matter" and "form." For Eucharist, the "matter" is clearly bread and wine; for Baptism, clearly water. For the sacrament of Penance, the act of expressing repentence is the matter or the visible sign. The form is the words of absolution pronounced by the priest.

Just as the "public" form had unintended consequences, so too did the "private" form. The sacrament lost its ecclesial and social character. It was called "Confession" and meant specifically the listing of sins, a title that referred to only one part of the conversion process of turning away from sin and turning back to God. It seemed to make the sinner the "active" person instead of celebrating the saving act of Christ.

The renewal of the sacrament of Penance and Reconciliation sought to restore the communal nature of sin and to emphasize that penance is not a private act but a lifelong process. Today, many parishes offer communal penance services during which private confession is offered and

Spotlight on the *Catechism*

"Interior repentance is a radical reorientation of our whole life, a return, a conversion to God with all our heart, an end of sin, a turning away from evil, with repugnance toward the evil actions we have committed. At the same time it entails the desire and resolution to change one's life, with hope in God's mercy and trust in the help of his grace."

Catechism of the Catholic Church, 1431

encouraged. "Sin should never be understood as a private or personal matter, because it harms our relationship with others and may even break our loving communion with the Church. The Sacrament of Penance repairs this break and has a renewing effect on the vitality of the Church itself" (*USCCA*, p. 242).

Pondering the Word

A man had two sons

Luke 15:11-32

Take a few minutes to savor a word, a phrase, a question, or a feeling that rises up in you. Reflect on this quietly or share it aloud.

Sharing Question

• When and how have I experienced God's unconditional mercy and forgiveness as did the Prodigal Son? When have I felt or behaved like the elder son?

Reflection 2

Sin and forgiveness

The story of the Prodigal Son is a remarkable parable of God's merciful love. It is also a story of the capacity for the human heart to undergo a total transformation through the power of the Holy Spirit. This transformation, or conversion, is the first step toward being reconciled with God, and our sisters and brothers in Christ. Oftentimes, like the younger son in the Gospel story, we need to be brought very low before we participate with the Holy Spirit and make the radical decision to return home, to choose life instead of death. In the New Testament this change of mind and heart is called *metanoia*. It signifies turning toward God, enabling us to offer confession, which "liberates us from sins that trouble our hearts and makes it possible to be reconciled to God and others. We are asked to look into our souls and, with an honest and unblinking gaze, identify our sins. This opens our minds and hearts to God, moves us toward communion with the Church, and offers us a new future" (*USCCA*, p. 238).

In the Scripture reading, we see a conversion journey being undertaken by the repentant son, who offers these words of confession, "Father, I have sinned against heaven and against you.

I no longer deserve to be called your son." His words acknowledge that he has behaved as is if he is no longer a son of the father. Asking to be a servant rather than a son is an act of humility and penance.

In the Sacrament of Penance and Reconciliation, we recognize our sinfulness and begin the journey back to God. But unlike the Prodigal Son, who did not know how or even if he would be received, we can have "confidence in God's mercy." We can look forward to the "party" that we are invited to in the celebration of the Eucharist, just as Cardinal Bernardin invited Steven Cook to celebrate the Eucharist following their reconciliation. Scripture reminds us that when God finds the one who is lost it is a cause for rejoicing. This is what the Sacrament of Penance and Reconciliation is, a celebration offered through the lavish love of our God who calls us continually to return home.

The United States Catechism for Adults explains that "conversion of heart is the beginning of our journey back to God. Liturgically this happens in the Sacrament of Penance" (*USCCA*, p. 237). Within the sacrament there are two essentials: "the acts of the penitent and the acts of Christ through the ministry of the Church" (*USCCA*, p. 237). Contrition and confession are the actions of the penitent. Absolution is the action of the priest who pardons the penitent through the power of Christ entrusted to the Church.

Conversion is a lifelong process made evident by a change in our actions, and both are made possible only through the grace of God (*USCCA*, p. 237). The Church recommends that we receive this sacrament often, rather than wait until we hit rock bottom, because regular confession "helps us form our consciences' fight against evil tendencies, let ourselves be healed by Christ and progress in the life of the Spirit" (*CCC*, 1458). The sacrament of Reconciliation challenges

Need for Forgiveness

"What happens in the Sacrament of Penance and Reconciliation is almost more than one could imagine. If we could meet Jesus today, we would expect to be received with love and compassion, because he is perfect and knows what it is to forgive. Instead, we confess to an ordinary human being who represents Jesus Christ sacramentally. We can expect the priest to receive us with love and care and compassion as well—not because he is sinless, but because he knows what it is to need forgiveness. God transforms even our human frailty into the medium of life-giving grace."

USCCB Subcommittee
for the Jubilee Year 2000,
*Jubilee 2000, A Year of the Lord's Favor:
A Reflection on Forgiveness
and Reconciliation*, 9

us to strive for holiness, to live with integrity and justice, and to offer forgiveness to others. We are called to be aware of sin in our personal lives and our implication in social sin. No sin is purely personal because others are always harmed by our sins. In addition, our society produces unjust laws and oppressive institutions. These "structures of sin" are an expression and effect of personal sins; further, they lead victims to do evil (*USCCA*, p. 528).

The Word of God leads us to this depth of awareness. "The New Testament is filled with calls to conversion and repentance, which need to be heard in our culture today. 'If we say, "We are without sin," we deceive ourselves, and the truth is not in us. If we acknowledge our sins, he is faithful and just and will forgive our sins and cleanse us from every wrong-doing' (1 John 1:8-9)" (*USCCA*, pp. 242-243).

Sharing Our Faith

- What evidence do I see of the reality of social sin in the world today?

- Consider how sin and/or reconciliation have affected a community of which you were a part. Share your thoughts.

- What would help me discern what needs forgiveness/conversion in my life? How can Scripture help me in this discernment?

- How would you explain this sacrament to others, especially people of other faiths? Which of the elements of the sacrament would you stress most?

- Whom do I need to forgive and how will I forgive him or her?

Living the Good News

Determine a specific action (individual or group) that flows from your sharing. This should be your primary consideration.

When choosing an individual action, determine what you will do and share it with the group. When choosing a group action, determine who will take responsibility for different aspects of action.

The following are secondary suggestions:

- Set aside a time to read the beatitudes and then make a thorough examination of your conscience.

- Celebrate the sacrament of Penance and Reconciliation this week.

- Contact someone you have offended, and if necessary, make restitution to that person.

- Join with members of your parish to fight evil in the world through ministries of education and action; such as pro-life, food bank, youth and young adult initiatives.

In light of this session, this week I commit to:

_____

_____

Lifting Our Hearts

Offer spontaneous prayers, asking forgiveness from God.

Leader	Lord Jesus, you came to gather the nations into the peace of God's kingdom: Lord, have mercy.
All	**Lord, have mercy.**
Leader	You come in word and sacrament to strengthen us in holiness: Christ, have mercy.
All	**Christ, have mercy.**
Leader	You will come again in glory with salvation for your people: Lord, have mercy.
All	**Lord, have mercy.**

(Litany of Praise, Penitential Rite)

Looking Ahead

- Prepare for your next session by prayerfully reading and studying:
  - Session 8: Anointing of the Sick: Healed and Forgiven;
  - Scripture: James 5:14-16;
  - pages 249-259 from Chapter 19, "Anointing the Sick and Dying," in the *United States Catholic Catechism for Adults;*
  - paragraphs 1499-1532 of the *Catechism of the Catholic Church.*
- Remember to use RENEWING FAMILY FAITH and its helpful suggestions on how to extend the fruits of your sharing beyond your group, especially to your families (see pages 96-97).

Anointing of the Sick:
Healed and Forgiven

Suggested Environment

Bible, candle, and a small table on which a Bible may be enthroned. Consider decorating the table with colors of the liturgical year and symbols of Anointing of the Sick such as oil, a stole and a pyx.

In addition it is suggested that the Catechism of the Catholic Church (CCC) *and the* United States Catholic Catechism for Adults (USCCA) *be available.*

Begin with a quiet, reflective atmosphere.

Lifting Our Hearts

Song Suggestion

"Every Tear We Cry," Mark LeVang
(RENEW/White Dove/OCP)

Prayer

Have someone in the group read Psalm 27 from the Bible. After each verse the entire group responds:

**Trust in God, and be of good courage;
let your heart take courage, yes, trust in God.**

Sharing Our Good News

The leader invites members of the group to share how they lived the Good News since their last meeting.

Reflection 1

Sacrament of healing

Times were exceptionally tough for Jake's family: The business was failing. Cheap look-alike products made with inferior materials were flooding the market and his customers were blaming him when these poorly manufactured items failed.

As they poured over the bills, Jake's wife Tammy noticed a swelling on his neck. "What's that? It looks like a lump!"

> "The sick person will be saved by a personal faith and the faith of the church, which looks back to the death and resurrection of Christ, the source of the sacrament's power and looks ahead to the future kingdom that is pledged in the sacraments."
>
> *Pastoral Care of the Sick:*
> *Rites of Anointing and Viaticum, 7*

"Yeah, noticed it while I was shaving. It just popped up over night. I called the doctor. I was going to tell you. I have an appointment tomorrow."

The following Friday, Jake was diagnosed with Hodgkin's lymphoma and scheduled for surgery. He and his wife confided in the priest, who arranged to celebrate the sacrament of the sick on Sunday during Mass.

Sharing the story with family and friends afterwards, Jake said, "I went to Mass full of anxiety, full of worries. What would happen to Tammy and our son Matt, a college student? Who would provide for them if something happened to me? Even our house is mortgaged. I prayed for strength, but couldn't feel a thing. Then, when I went up to be anointed and Father prayed over me and made the sign of the cross with the oil on me, a calm came over me. I could feel the power of the prayer of the whole congregation gathered around us at the altar, and I heard in my heart, 'Jake, it's going to be OK.' Somehow I knew at that moment that the surgery would be OK, that the cancer would be OK, the business and my family would be OK. I'm a life-long Catholic and had studied about the sacrament, but that was when I really understood what 'grace of the sacrament' means."

Like most people with cancer, Jake went for follow-up treatment after the surgery and suffered from the effects, but he was at peace. Every now and then, he'd re-tell the story of his anointing, saying, "I know I can get through this and even if I don't recover, I just know it will be OK."

When he received the sacrament of the Anointing of the Sick, Jake experienced healing—he was relieved of his worries about himself and his family. The sacrament did not reveal the future; he didn't know what would happen to his wife and children. But he was able to move from fear and anxiety to trusting in the Lord.

Healing in Jesus' ministry came through the spoken word and the laying on of hands. As God incarnate he understood the human need for another's touch or presence, the isolation of being alone, and the fear of suffering. Jesus also understood that human beings are more than just their physical bodies. Scripture is filled with stories of his healing ministry, stories which show him healing body and soul, sometimes with words, sometimes with a touch, oftentimes emphasizing the role of faith and forgiveness in the healing process.

Spotlight on the *Catechism*

"When the Sacrament of Anointing of the Sick is given, the hoped-for effect is that, if it be God's will, the person be physically healed of illness. But even if there is no physical healing, the primary effect of the Sacrament is a spiritual healing by which the sick person receives the Holy Spirit's gift of peace and courage to deal with the difficulties that accompany serious illness or the frailty of old age. The Holy Spirit renews our faith in God and helps us withstand the temptations of the Evil One to be discouraged and despairing in the face of suffering and death. Also, a sick person's sins are forgiven if he or she was not able to go to Confession prior to the celebration of the Sacrament of the Anointing of the Sick."

United States Catholic Catechism for Adults, p. 254

Jesus' healing of others was about making those who were sick whole. He touched the eyes of the blind men, saying "let it be done for you according to your faith" (Matthew 9:29). He assured the woman with the hemorrhage, "Daughter, your faith has saved you. Go in peace and be cured of your affliction" (Mark 5:34). On another occasion, when the friends of a paralyzed man go so far as to cut a hole in the roof of the house and lower their friend down to where the Lord is teaching, Jesus responds to the faith of the friends by first saying to the young man, "Child, your sins are forgiven" (Mark 2:5). Only then did Jesus tell him to get up, take his mat and go home, and the man was healed.

The healing ministry was also part of the disciples' call. Scripture tells us that after Jesus sent them out two by two, "they anointed with oil many who were sick and cured them" (Mark 6: 13). After Jesus' death, resurrection and ascension, the disciples continued his healing ministry, following in the footsteps of Christ who was the sacrament of God's healing power. It is our mission, as Church, to continue this ministry and be a sacrament of healing as well.

Pondering the Word

Is anyone among you sick?

James 5:14-16

Take a few minutes to savor a word, a phrase, a question, or a feeling that rises up in you. Reflect on this quietly or share it aloud.

Sharing Question

- Have I ever received the Anointing of the Sick or been with someone who has? What was the experience like for me?

Reflection 2

Celebration of faith

The Letter of James highlights three essential elements of the Sacrament of Anointing: the laying on of hands, anointing with oil, and the prayer of faith. These elements express and address our humanity through the power of touch and symbol, and the expression of our faith in the God who loves us. The letter directs us to turn to the presbyters, the priests, who administer the sacrament, and to the community for healing and support.

We are already accustomed to asking members of our faith community to pray for us or for our loved ones, but the Letter of James asks for something more; a humility that allows us to confess our sins to each other, to seek and offer forgiveness that not only benefits us as individuals but is a source of spiritual growth for the community as well.

During the third century, the emphasis of this sacrament shifted from healing to one of confession and forgiveness. Those who were ill saw the sacrament as their final opportunity to reconcile themselves with God, often postponing the sacrament until death was imminent. During the Middle Ages the common term for the sacrament became Extreme Unction, or Last Rites, and was reserved for those who were close to death. This became the norm until the Second Vatican Council called for a renewal of the sacrament based on its original intent of strengthening and healing, through the power of the Holy Spirit, all those who were seriously ill in body and soul.

The renewal of the sacrament also restored the focus of the sacrament as a liturgical and communal celebration, rather than a private ritual;

one that is appropriately celebrated within "the Eucharist, the memorial of the Lord's Passover … The celebration of the sacrament can be preceded by the sacrament of Penance and followed by the sacrament of the Eucharist. As the sacrament of Christ's Passover the Eucharist should always be the last sacrament of the earthly journey, the 'viaticum' for 'passing over' to eternal life" (*CCC*, 1517).

If possible, Anointing of the Sick should not be delayed until the sick person is too frail to play a part in it. If the person is near death, he or she may not even be aware of what is happening. "If a sick person who received this anointing recovers his health, he can in the case of another grave illness receive this sacrament again. If during the same illness the person's condition becomes more serious, the sacrament may be repeated. It is fitting to receive the Anointing of the Sick just prior to a serious operation. The same holds for the elderly whose frailty becomes more pronounced" (*CCC*, 1515).

When possible, the sacrament should be integrated into the local Christian community. This gathering should include family, neighbors and friends. Many parishes have gatherings in their churches on Sundays throughout the year where the Anointing of the Sick is celebrated as part of the ordinary Sunday celebration.

Spotlight on the *Catechism*

"The special grace of the sacrament of the Anointing of the Sick has as its effects:

- the uniting of the sick person to the passion of Christ, for his own good and that of the whole Church;

- the strengthening, peace, and courage to endure in a Christian manner the sufferings of illness or old age;

- the forgiveness of sins, if the sick person was not able to obtain it through the sacrament of Penance;

- the restoration of health, if it is conducive to the salvation of his soul;

- the preparation for passing over to eternal life."

Catechism of the Catholic Church, 1532

With a renewed understanding of the communal celebration of Anointing of the Sick, we follow the example of those whose faith in Jesus spurred them to bring their sick friend to him for healing. We are each called to be sacraments, signs of God's love, to others, and to bring others to Christ to be healed in body, mind and spirit.

As a celebration of faith, Anointing of the Sick is a sacrament that truly reflects the compassionate heart of Jesus who had a special love for the sick and suffering. Jesus entered into our suffering and understood our needs. His example of healing served to teach the disciples that times of carrying our cross are times when we need to be strengthened in faith and trust in God. His words encourage us to see our suffering in the light of his cross. Jesus entered into our human condition, became flesh and blood, because God loves us. Through the power of the Holy Spirit, the Sacrament of the Anointing of the Sick provides us with the strength and courage to enter in to Christ's life, death, and resurrection with a similar love. It helps us make meaning of suffering, illness, aging, healing and death in the light of our Christian faith.

> "When the church cares for the sick, it serves Christ himself in the suffering members of his Mystical Body."
>
> *Pastoral Care of the Sick: Rites of Anointing and Viaticum*

Sharing Our Faith

- Thinking back to a time of being sick or injured, where I have found God in this experience?

- How has my understanding of the sacrament of Anointing the Sick changed, or not, over the years?

- In what ways have I brought others to Jesus for healing?

- How can I better prepare for my own death?

Living the Good News

Determine a specific action (individual or group) that flows from your sharing. This should be your primary consideration for choosing an action.

If choosing an individual action, determine what you will do and share it with the group. If choosing a group action, determine who will take responsibility for different aspects of the action.

The following are secondary suggestions:

- Pray for those who are ill or dying.

- Make contact this week through phone, letter, e-mail, or home visit to a person who is sick.

- Offer your assistance at a local nursing home.

- Attend or help organize a communal Anointing of the Sick in your parish or in a nursing home to support those who are sick or suffering.

- Encourage someone who is ill or elderly to receive the sacrament of the Anointing of the Sick.

- Participate in political action that will assist the handicapped and elderly who may not be able to speak for themselves.

In light of this session, this week I commit to:

_____

_____

Lifting Our Hearts

Offer spontaneous prayers for those who are seriously ill or dying.

Invite one person to read Philippians 4:4-7.

Then pray together
God, give us your peace.
Always let us be open to your will.
When the time comes and you call us home,
let us say unreservedly, "Yes, my God, I am ready.
Just be with me, and welcome me home. Amen."

Looking Ahead

- Prepare for your next session by prayerfully reading and studying:

  - Session 9: Holy Orders: Called to Serve;

  - Scripture: Hebrews 5:1-10;

  - pages 261-275 from Chapter 19, "Holy Orders," in the *United States Catholic Catechism for Adults;*

  - paragraphs 1536-1600 of the *Catechism of the Catholic Church.*

- Remember to use RENEWING FAMILY FAITH and its helpful suggestions on how to extend the fruits of your sharing beyond your group, especially to your families (see pages 96-97).

Holy Orders:
Called to Serve

Suggested Environment

Bible, candle, and a small table on which a Bible may be enthroned. Consider decorating the table with colors of the liturgical year and symbols of Holy Orders, such as oil, a stole, a miter, bread and wine, a copy of the Roman Missal *and the* Book of the Gospels.

In addition it is suggested that the Catechism of the Catholic Church (CCC) *and the* United States Catholic Catechism for Adults (USCCA) *be available.*

Begin with a quiet, reflective atmosphere.

Lifting Our Hearts

Song Suggestion

"I Commit My Life to You," Mark LeVang and Norma Catherine (RENEW/White Dove/OCP)

Prayer

Prayer for Our Priests, Deacons, and Bishops

Pray together

Lord, our God and Father,
we thank you for the deacons, priests, and bishops
whom you have called
from among the people of God to serve.

Through your Spirit
give them good health,
peace and joy in their
diaconal, priestly, and Episcopal ministries.

Strengthen them for faithful service
within your Church

so that they may ardently and gently
minister your mysteries,
that your faithful people
may grow in the knowledge of your love
and become holy in mind and heart and action.

We ask this in the name of your Son Jesus,
eternal High Priest and
through the power of your Holy Spirit. Amen.

Sharing Our Good News

The leader invites members of the group to share how they lived the Good News since their last meeting.

Reflection 1

A new order

Oscar Romero's appointment as archbishop of San Salvador in 1977 was welcomed by the El Salvadoran government. At the time, the Church hierarchy was aligned with the country's wealthy landowning families and the military was trying to suppress a land reform rebellion. Because of the new archbishop's reputation as a quiet and conservative priest, he was viewed as someone who would not make waves. But Archbishop Romero gradually became aware of the suffering of the people of El Salvador. He began to see his country and his Church differently. The poor were suffering and the priests and religious who were trying to help them were being kidnapped, tortured, and murdered. When a close friend, a Jesuit priest, was assassinated along with an elderly man and a young boy, the archbishop demanded that the government investigate but he was ignored. The archbishop began to preach and give radio addresses about the repression of the people and the atrocities that were being committed against the Church. He called for international intervention and ordered soldiers to stop violating the human rights of the people. As a result, he was assassinated while celebrating Mass on March 24, 1980. Once viewed as a pious but harmless Church bureaucrat, Archbishop Romero is remembered for his solidarity with the poor and his courageous, prophetic stance on behalf of justice, truth, and peace.

In the Old Testament, there was clearly a priesthood of the Old Covenant. Of the twelve tribes of Israel, the tribe of Levi was set aside for liturgical service. As priests, they were appointed to act on behalf of the community in their relationship with God and to offer gifts and sacrifices to God for the community (CCC, 1539). When Jesus came into the world, this priesthood had become focused mostly on temple activities and rituals, along with the teaching and application of the commandments. At the time of Jesus, Pharisees and other groups disputed the priestly prerogative of teaching and interpreting the commandments.

As prefigured in the Old Testament, Jesus came as the high priest who established a New Covenant with God. The early Christian community, building on the experience of the Israelites and the words of Jesus, initiated various ministries of service in the early Church. Although shaped by an understanding of the priesthood of the Old Covenant, the Church saw these ministries as the priesthood of the New Covenant. It differed from the levitical priesthood that was passed down in the male line (see the reference to the order of Melchizedek, a king who had no lineage, in Hebrews 7:1-28). It primarily came from their relationship with Christ, who taught them a new order. Priesthood was to be about service. It was to be about the willingness to suffer and die and then be raised up. Before his death, Archbishop Romero knew he was targeted and spoke publicly about his belief that new life would come to his country as a result of the shedding of his blood. For Archbishop Romero, as for Jesus, priesthood was about being willing to be the least in order to be the greatest. Listen to the instruction given to the Hebrews on priesthood.

Pondering the Word

Every high priest is taken from among mortals

Hebrews 5:1-10

Take a few minutes to savor a word, a phrase, a question, or a feeling that rises up in you. Reflect on this quietly or share it aloud.

Spotlight on the *Catechism*

"The priesthood has a sacramental nature. The priest is a sign of what is happening. Sacramental signs represent what they signify by a natural resemblance. This resemblance is as true for persons as for things. When the priest acts in the person of Christ, he takes on the role of Christ, to the point of being his representative. He is a sign of what is happening and must be a sign that is recognizable, which the faithful can see with ease."

United States Catholic Catechism for Adults, p. 268

Sharing Questions

• Jesus established a "new order" of priesthood based on service to others. In what ways have members of the ordained ministry served me? If I am ordained, how have I best served others?

Reflection 2

Ordained ministry

There are two forms of participation in the priesthood of Jesus that flow from the baptismal grace of all Christians. The first is the common priesthood to which all who are baptized and confirmed are consecrated. The second is the ministerial priesthood, of bishops and priests. "The ministerial priesthood is at the service of the common priesthood … a means by which Christ unceasingly builds up and leads his Church" (*CCC*, 1547; see also *CCC*, 1548).

When a man is ordained, "the presence of Christ as head of the Church is made visible in the midst of the community of believers (cf. *Lumen gentium*, 21)" (*CCC*, 1549). Through the grace of the Holy Spirit, the man who is ordained is configured to Christ as Priest, Teacher, and Pastor. "The risen Christ, by giving the Holy Spirit to the apostles, entrusted to them his power of sanctifying (cf. John 20:21-23): they became sacramental signs of Christ. By the power of the same Holy Spirit they entrusted this power to their successors" (*CCC*, 1087). This is what we mean by "apostolic succession."

When a man is called to priesthood, he is called to a life of service to God and to the community of believers. Priesthood presents a unique call to become like Jesus and to live out concretely the values of Jesus (*CCC*, 1551). To be called to priesthood is to be called to a life of love. To be called to priesthood is, when presenting to God the prayer of the Church, and above all when presiding at the Eucharist, to be called to act in the name of the whole Church (*CCC*, 1552). To be a minister of Christ is to be a minister of the Church (*CCC*, 1553). "The ordained are called to a holiness of life and an attitude of humility that conforms them to Christ whose priesthood they share" (*USCCA*, p. 265).

The vocation to the priesthood is a calling to a deep commitment to the gospel. The ordained's call is to cherish and to be faithful to the call to discipleship to Jesus Christ in all his ministry (*CCC*, 1550). Even though the ordained, like all believers, is weak and sinful, his failures do not invalidate the effects of the sacraments he administers because it is ultimately Christ who acts through the sacraments.

There are three degrees of ordained ministry: of these, bishops and priests share in the ministerial priesthood; deacons share in a ministry of service. All three are conferred by what we call "ordination," that is the sacrament of Holy Orders. The ordination of bishops, priests, or deacons, which is celebrated after the Liturgy of the Word and before the eucharistic liturgy, follows the same movement. The sacrament itself is conveyed by the laying on of hands and the solemn prayer calling for the graces of the Spirit that will be required for ministry (*CCC*, 1573-1574).

As successors of the Apostles, bishops receive the fullness of the sacrament of Holy Orders and become the leaders of their local church (diocese) in the person of Christ. Through the sacrament, bishops receive the grace "to teach in the name of Christ; to sanctify the Church through the celebration of the Sacraments; to guide, govern, and defend the Church; and to be a sign of the unity of the Church" (*USCCA*, p. 271). Bishops, who are the legitimate successors of the Apostles, are the only ministers who may ordain deacons, priests, or other bishops and are entrusted with the responsibility of calling forth suitable men from among the common priesthood of the faithful to ordained service to the Church.

Through ordination and the grace of the Holy Spirit, priests become co-workers with the bishop, assuming the pastoral care of parishes or ministries to which the bishop assigns them. Before a man is ordained as a priest, he is ordained to the transitional diaconate. Holy Orders gives a priest the grace "to proclaim the Gospel and preach, to celebrate the Sacraments (except Holy Orders), and to shepherd the people entrusted to him" (*USCCA*, p. 271).

The role of the priest makes possible the communion of the baptized with Christ through the celebration of Eucharist, strengthening them

Spotlight on the *Catechism*

"The Sacrament of Holy Orders, like that of Baptism and Confirmation, confers an indelible or permanent character on the recipient. This means that this Sacrament cannot be received again. The indelible character is a reminder to the bishop, priest, or deacon that the vocation and mission he received on the day of his ordination marks him permanently. Like Baptism and Confirmation, which also confer a permanent character, Holy Orders is never repeated."

United States Catholic Catechism for Adults, p. 271

Almighty God, …

You make the Church, Christ's body,

Grow to its full stature as a new and greater temple.

You enrich it with every kind of grace

And perfect it with a diversity of members

To serve the whole body

in a wonderful pattern of unity.

You established a threefold ministry

of worship and service,

For the glory of your name.

Roman Pontifical, Ordination of Deacons, 21,
Prayer of Consecration

in their mission of service to the world. Celebrating the Eucharist is also the source of great joy in the life of the priest. The priest builds up the community of the faithful. He gathers them in prayer, leads them to encounter God through the sacraments, inspires and challenges them to live the values of the Gospel through his preaching, and leads them to the heavenly Jerusalem as a shepherd leads his flock.

A deacon is ordained not to the ministerial priesthood but to the ministry of service. "Through ordination the deacon is conformed to Christ, who came to serve, not to be served" (*USCCA*, p. 266). Married and unmarried men may be ordained to the permanent diaconate. If married, a deacon's wife is called to support her husband's ministry. Deacons proclaim the Gospel, preach the homily, assist the bishop or priest in the celebration of the Eucharist, assist at and bless marriages, and preside at funerals. In addition, they serve the community through works of charity. The order of diaconate as a permanent ministry (not just as a transition to priesthood) fell into disuse during the Middle Ages. It was restored by the Second Vatican Council liturgical renewal (see *Lumen gentium*, 29). Among the reasons for its re-establishment were the desires to restore the full complement of active apostolic ministries to the Church and to integrate and strengthen with sacramental ordination and grace those who were exercising diaconal functions. In addition, deacons could perform many of the functions of priests so it would help alleviate the shortage of priests in various parts of the world.

The sacramental life of the Church has been preserved and passed on to us through the sacrament of Holy Orders. We are faced with a crisis of vocations to priesthood in our nation and in many parts of the world today, endangering the availability of the sacraments to the people of God. Besides asking the Lord of the harvest to send forth laborers to his harvest, we need to be proactive in promoting vocations to the priesthood. We need to encourage the young to recognize and place their gifts at the service of the community.

We all share the responsibility to encourage a response to God's call to the priesthood for the good of our own spiritual lives and that of the Church.

Sharing Our Faith

- How do I relate with the deacons, priests and bishop in my diocese or parish? If I am ordained, how do I relate with those who are not?

- What kind of support can I give to those who are ordained to the diaconate, priesthood, and episcopacy? If I am ordained, what kind of support do I need from the community?

- How can I encourage young men to consider a vocation to the priesthood or the permanent diaconate?

Living the Good News

Determine a specific action (individual or group) that flows from your sharing. This should be your primary consideration for choosing an action.

If choosing an individual action, determine what you will do and share it with the group. If choosing a group action, determine who will take responsibility for different aspects of the action.

The following are secondary suggestions:

- Suggest that members of the group plan to take part in an ordination liturgy the next time you have the opportunity. Then arrange a faith-sharing session on how the prayers, rites, and symbols used in the celebration express what the ordained ministry is meant to be.

- Invite a priest or deacon to share the meaning of his call to Holy Orders with you.

- Offer some concrete support to deacons, priests, and bishops in your diocese or parish. Do not overlook the importance of prayer.

- Engage young men to reflect about whether they feel called to the life of ordained priesthood. Contact your diocesan vocation office for materials, advice, etc.

In light of this session, this week I commit to:

_____

_____

Lifting Our Hearts

Offer spontaneous prayers for those who have been ordained or are preparing for ordination.

Invite one person to pray the following:

My dearest Lord,
Be a bright flame
Before me,
Be a guiding star
Above me,
Be a smooth path
Beneath me,
Be a kindly shepherd
Behind me,
Today and for ever more.

(Adapted from St. Columba, Abbot and Missionary, AD 521-597)

Pray together

**Gracious God,
bless us with joy and gratitude,
that we may worship you with all our heart,
with all our mind, body, and soul.**

**Bless those who have been called
to be your special anointed ones,
and keep them holy.**

We ask this in Jesus' name. Amen.

Looking Ahead

- Prepare for your next session by prayerfully reading and studying:
  - Session 10: Matrimony: Covenant of Love;
  - Scripture: 1 John 4:7-21;
  - pages 277-292 from Chapter 21, "The Sacrament of Marriage," in the *United States Catholic Catechism for Adults;*
  - paragraphs 1601-1666 of the *Catechism of the Catholic Church.*
- Remember to use RENEWING FAMILY FAITH and its helpful suggestions on how to extend the fruits of your sharing beyond your group, especially to your families (see pages 96-97).

Matrimony:
Covenant of Love

Suggested Environment

Bible, candle, and a small table on which a Bible may be enthroned. Consider decorating the table with colors of the liturgical year and other symbols of faith.

In addition it is suggested that the Catechism of the Catholic Church (CCC) *and the* United States Catholic Catechism for Adults (USCCA) *be available.*

Begin with a quiet, reflective atmosphere.

Lifting Our Hearts

Song Suggestion

"We Come Together," Michael Semana and Norma Catherine (White Dove/OCP/RENEW)

Prayer

Prayer for Marriage

Leader	God our Father, we give you thanks for the gift of marriage: the bond of life and love, and the font of the family.
Side 1	The love of husband and wife enriches your Church with children, fills the world with a multitude of spiritual fruitfulness and service, and is the sign of the love of your Son, Jesus Christ, for his Church.
Side 2	The grace of Jesus flowed forth at Cana at the request of the Blessed Mother.

May your Son, through the intercession of Mary,
pour out upon us a new measure
of the Gifts of the Holy Spirit
as we join with all people of good will
to promote and protect the unique beauty of marriage.

Side 1   May your Holy Spirit enlighten our society
to treasure the heroic love of husband and wife,
and guide our leaders to sustain and protect
the singular place of mothers and fathers
in the lives of their children.

Side 2   Father, we ask that our prayers be joined
to those of the Virgin Mary,
that your Word may transform our service so as to
safeguard the incomparable splendor of marriage.

All   **We ask all these things through Christ our Lord,
Amen.**

Saints Joachim and Anne, pray for us.

(United States Conference of Catholic Bishops)

Sharing Our Good News

The leader invites members of the group to share how they lived the Good News since their last meeting.

Reflection 1

Love one another

When Jim and Laura married they looked forward to having a large family. By the time they were married they already had many nieces and nephews, and they were excited to have children of their own. When Laura realized she was pregnant after six months of marriage, she couldn't wait to share the news with Jim. They began to convert their extra bedroom into a nursery. But a few months into the pregnancy Laura experienced a miscarriage. Laura and Jim were devastated. Laura had been careful to follow her doctor's instructions—she had stopped drinking coffee and alcohol, and was taking prenatal vitamins as prescribed. She couldn't understand what had gone wrong, and she blamed herself for the miscarriage. Jim, too, was disappointed, but tried to reassure his wife that it was not her fault. As the years went on, Laura and Jim experienced numerous miscarriages. They were honest with each other about their sorrow, but they focused their energy on helping to raise the many children in their extended family.

Scripture's vision of the beginning of time depicts the creation of man and woman, together and for each other, in the image and likeness of God (Genesis 1:26-24). Scripture's vision of the end of time presents the marriage feast of the Lamb (Revelation 19:7, 9). These two marriages stand like bookends to the whole of human history, inviting us to see love as underpinning the very meaning of our existence. The whole of Scripture is the story of God's loving relationship with humankind, a relationship that is often expressed in the word "covenant."

Genesis chapter 1 is a meditation, through the eyes of faith, on the origin of humanity, on our own origin, and sees the very fact that we are male and female as telling us something essential about God. Man and woman complement each other, achieving fullness only in mutual love, in mutual self-giving—a love that in turn gives birth to new life. Marriage—as a declaration and an act of love—is a privileged moment in human life where we glimpse something of God's unconditional love for us. This is why marriage so richly deserves the title "sacrament."

When Jesus is challenged by some Pharisees about marriage and divorce, it is to this founding vision of Genesis that he turns. Jesus answers the question on whether divorce is lawful by saying: "Have you not read that from the beginning the Creator 'made them male and female' and said, 'For this reason a man shall leave his father and mother and be joined to his wife, and the two shall become one flesh'? So they are no longer two, but one flesh. Therefore, what God has joined together, no human being must separate" (Matthew 19:3-6; *USCCA*, page 280).

Jesus was replying to a question about Jewish marriage. History shows it took time for polygamy to be replaced by monogamy. This social change was matched by a developing idea of "covenant" as the relationship between God and the people. A covenant is more than a contract, more than an arrangement of convenience: Covenant implies total, unconditional loving. This is how God offers himself to his people, and looks for love freely given in return. So, too marriage came to be seen as more than a contract. By giving love to each other, the couple enters into a covenant, and this covenant of love they share is a mirror of God's love for his people.

The prophets (Hosea, Isaiah, Jeremiah, and Ezechiel) explicitly invite us to see God's covenant with his people in terms of the love of husband and wife. With one key difference: Even if the people fail (something the prophets find themselves obliged to say again and again as the people prove to be unfaithful), God remains ever faithful.

It is this tradition of a full and wholesome vision of human love that Jesus evokes, not just in what he says but in what he does. On the last night of his earthly life, Jesus shares the cup of wine and with it entrusts to us "the new covenant"; in John's Gospel, Christ's ministry begins at a marriage, the wedding at Cana. It is already a celebration, but the presence of Jesus lifts it out of the ordinary, as water becomes wine, wine of superlative quality (*CCC*, 1613; *USCCA*, p. 280)! John's Gospel will show that earthly ministry ending with blood and water flowing from the side of Christ. The Church has long interpreted the subtle inter-relation of the two passages from John's Gospel to see the cross as the moment of "marriage" of Christ and the Church.

"It was from his side that Christ formed the Church, just as from the side of Adam Eve was formed. 'Bone of my bone, flesh of my flesh …' just as God took a rib from Adam's side as he slept and formed woman, so Christ, while he slept the sleep of death on the cross, gave us blood and water from his side and formed the Church. Do you not see how Christ has united his bride to himself?" (John Chrysostom, *Catechesis* 3)

This key idea is expressed even more directly in the Letter to the Ephesians. Paul quotes from Genesis, "For this reason a man must leave his father and mother and be joined to his wife, and the two will become one body" (Genesis 2:24). Then he explains: "This mystery has many implications, but I am saying it applies to Christ and the Church" (Ephesians 5:32).

"Mystery," as we have seen in previous sessions, is the same word as "sacrament." Marriage, Paul is saying, has many implications; for those who are members of Christ's body, it has particular "sacramental" significance. The covenant that Christians establish with each other in marriage speaks not just of their loving relationship, but of the relationship between Christ and the Church —in particular, Christ's complete giving of himself.

To be holy is to be like God; the best way to become like God is to become people of love. The love of a married couple is a reflection, a "sacrament" of God's love. But sacraments are more than passive signs; they actively make happen what they symbolize. Marriage is not just the promises of one human partner to another; it is also God's promise that in their mutual love the couple can be certain to find him.

So it is that the grace of the sacrament perfects the love of husband and wife. "Christ is the source of this grace and he dwells with the spouses to strengthen their covenant promises, to bear each other's burdens with forgiveness and kindness, and to experience ahead of time the 'wedding feast of the Lamb' (Revelation 19:9)" (*USCCA*, p. 285).

Pondering the Word

God is love

1 John 4:7-21

Take a few minutes to savor a word, a phrase, a question, or a feeling that rises up in you. Reflect on this quietly or share it aloud.

Sharing Question

• If I am married, how do I experience God's love through my husband or wife? If I am not married, how do I experience God's love through another person?

Reflection 2

Unselfish love

Within marriage, conjugal love should be an expression of the total love that two people have for each other and should be "at the service of life" (*CCC*, 1653). For serious reasons, a couple by mutual agreement may at times refrain from sexual union during fertile periods. Artificial means to prevent contraception are against Church teaching. The use of contraceptives may lead to a mentality and a culture that are opposed to Christian love. Sacrifice

Divorce and Pastoral Care

The Church's fidelity to Christ's teaching on marriage and against divorce does not imply insensitivity to the pain of the persons facing these unhappy situations. When divorce is the only possible recourse, the Church offers her support to those involved and encourages them to remain close to the Lord through frequent reception of the Sacraments, especially the Holy Eucharist. In the case of those who have divorced civilly and remarried, even though the Church considers the second marriage invalid, she does not want these Catholics to be alienated from her … [T]hey are encouraged to participate in the life of their parish communities and to attend the Sunday Eucharist, even though they cannot receive Holy Communion.

United States Catholic Catechism for Adults, pp. 287–288

A Declaration of Nullity (Annulment)

"The marriage of two baptized persons celebrated according to the norms of Church law is always presumed to be valid. When a marriage has broken down, this presumption remains in effect until the contrary is proven. The examination of the validity of a marriage is undertaken by a Church tribunal or court. When a Church court issues a declaration of nullity, … it does not mean that the children of the union are illegitimate. The declaration means that no sacramental bond—or, in the case of one party's being unbaptized, no natural bond—took place because at the time of the wedding, the standards for a valid marriage were not met. Grounds for a declaration of nullity (annulment) include flaws in the rite itself, in the legal capacity of the parties to marry (i.e., an "impediment"), or in the consent they gave—whether they were lacking in discretion or maturity of judgment or were marrying due to force or fear or with an intent to exclude fidelity or the commitment to a lifelong union or were placing unacceptable conditions on the marriage (cf. *CCC*, 1628-1629). Once a declaration of nullity has been granted, if there are no other restrictions, one or both of the parties are free to enter a sacramental marriage in the Catholic Church."

United States Catholic Catechism for Adults, pp. 288-289

and self-denial for the sake of one's spouse or children are at the heart of a happy and fulfilling marriage.

The forces of materialism, hedonism, and consumerism rampant in societies may easily infect a marriage relationship and encourage attitudes and decisions that ultimately doom it to failure. There is a mysterious dimension to our sexuality that does not follow reason or logic unless we impose them upon it. Sex is a powerful drive, capable of creating or destroying our family and all that is best about us.

The Church teaches that sexuality is all about faithfulness, commitment, and the expression of love. Frequently, sexuality is separated from love. When sex becomes more important than love, it can lead to the pursuit of selfish pleasure, dishonesty, betrayal, and broken commitments. If we do not reverence our sexuality, it can bring about our destruction. If we do not value our sexuality, we do not value ourselves.

The grace of the sacrament of Matrimony supports the couple's efforts to live chastely and the strong foundation of the family unity. Faithfulness, sensitivity, tenderness, and affection depend on our ability to control our sexual urges. Self-discipline and self-control are not easy; they do not just happen. They are learned through the painful process of practicing good habits like abstinence and rejecting bad habits like promiscuity.

When couples are blessed with children, they are responsible to be "the principal and first educators" of their children in the faith (*CCC*, 1653) in a "community of grace and prayer, a school of human virtues and of Christian charity" (*CCC*, 1666). As parents, we can teach our children about God from the moment we first hold them in our arms. For them, we are the first experience they have of a power greater than themselves, and we can mirror God's unconditional love and acceptance. Through our marital fidelity we model healthy male and female images for our children by providing the context for their physical, psychological, and spiritual development.

While procreation and education of children are the primary purposes of the family, John Paul II taught that the family also has an important social role. Family life is not intended to be "closed in on itself"; rather, "the family is by nature and vocation open to other families and to society" (*Familiaris consortio*, 42). Families are to devote themselves to social service activities especially on behalf of the poor, and to practice hospitality.

Today, more than ever, families are called to be places and centers for living and radiating faith. The Second Vatican Council called families "the Domestic Church" (*Lumen gentium*, 11). The home should be the first place where children learn about Christian life. Parents and children together learn about love and forgiveness. Because we live in a fractured society, we must remember those who do not have close families. It is so important for us today to create family wherever we are, to treat all human beings with love and respect. We are reminded of our great family that we call the Church. "No one is without a family in this world: the Church is a home and family for everyone, especially those who 'labor and are heavy laden'" (*Familiaris consortio*, 85; cf. Matthew 11:28) (*CCC*, 1658).

The sacrament of Matrimony ideally takes place during a eucharistic liturgy. Those being married are the ministers of Christ's grace and mutually confer the sacrament upon each other by expressing their consent in the presence of the Church (*CCC*, 1623). The necessary elements in celebrating the sacrament include: the freedom of consent, that is a free act of the will on the part of each of the parties, which involves a lifelong, exclusive commitment, and openness to children. A priest or deacon assists at the celebration and witnesses attest that marriage is an ecclesial reality (*CCC*, 1625-1631). In addition, "[s]o that the 'I do' of the spouses may be a free and responsible act and so that the marriage covenant may have solid and lasting human and Christian foundations, preparation for marriage is of prime importance" (*CCC*, 1632).

As married couples grow together, they should call upon the power of the Holy Spirit to help them in their relationship. The grace of the sacrament aims at creating deep personal unity; it demands indissolubility and faithfulness and is open to fertility (*CCC*, 1643, 1652). For love to grow, it is essential that each person knows the fidelity of the other. The fidelity of husband and wife is an earthly sign of God's faithful and unconditional love for his people (*CCC*, 1641-43).

Sharing Our Faith

- If I am married, what does the sacrament of Matrimony mean in my life? If not, what does it mean in the lives of my family or friends?

- If I have children, what graces are given to me to help me be a good parent? How have my spouse and I grown in the faith through our relationship?

Living the Good News

Determine a specific action (individual or group) that flows from your sharing. This should be your primary consideration for choosing an action.

If choosing an individual action, determine what you will do and share it with the group. If choosing a group action, determine who will take responsibility for different aspects of the action.

The following are secondary suggestions:

- Offer to assist in the marriage preparation program in your parish.

- If you are married, spend more time with your spouse and express your love.

- If you are experiencing tension or are struggling in your relationship, pray together for the power to work it out. Make a decision to seek help from a marriage counselor with solid gospel values.

- Whether you are married or not, express gratitude for your relationship to someone who has been a special friend in your life.

In light of this session, this week I commit to:

_____

_____

Lifting Our Hearts

Offer spontaneous prayers for those you love.

Pray the following prayer together:

A Prayer for Families

We bless your name, O Lord,
for sending your own incarnate Son,
to become part of a family,
so that, as he lived its life,
he would experience its worries and its joys.

We ask you, Lord,
to protect and watch over our families,
so that in the strength of your grace
our family members may enjoy prosperity,
possess the priceless gift of your peace,
and, as the Church alive in the home,
bear witness in this world to your glory.

We ask this through Christ our Lord. Amen.

(Adapted, United Stated Conference of Catholic Bishops)

Looking Ahead

- Prepare for your next session by prayerfully reading and studying:
    - Session 11: Sacramentals and Devotions: 'Pray at All Times';
    - Scripture: Matthew 5:1-12;
    - pages 293-303 from Chapter 22, "Sacramental and Popular Devotions," in the *United States Catholic Catechism for Adults;*
    - paragraphs 1667-1679 of the *Catechism of the Catholic Church.*
- Remember to use RENEWING FAMILY FAITH and its helpful suggestions on how to extend the fruits of your sharing beyond your group, especially to your families (see pages 96-97).

Sacramentals and Devotions: 'Pray at All Times'

Suggested Environment

Bible, candle, and a small table on which a Bible may be enthroned. Consider decorating the table with examples of sacramental objects such as rosary beads, holy water, prayer cards, medals and palm leaves.

In addition it is suggested that the Catechism of the Catholic Church (CCC) *and the* United States Catholic Catechism for Adults (USCCA) *be available.*

Begin with a quiet, reflective atmosphere.

Lifting Our Hearts

Song Suggestion

"We Walk By Faith," Marty Haugen (GIA)

Prayer

Litany of the Saints

Leader	Lord, have mercy on us.
All	**Lord, have mercy on us.**
Leader	Christ, have mercy on us.
All	**Christ, have mercy on us.**
Leader	Lord, have mercy on us.
All	**Lord, have mercy on us.**
Leader	Christ, hear us.
All	**Christ, graciously hear us.**
Leader	God, the Father of heaven,
All	**have mercy on us.**

Leader	God the Son, Redeemer of the world,
All	**have mercy on us.**
Leader	God the Holy Spirit,
All	**have mercy on us.**
Leader	Holy Trinity, one God,
All	**have mercy on us.**

Leader	Holy Mary,
All	**pray for us.**
Leader	Holy Mother of God,
All	**pray for us.**
Leader	Holy Virgin of virgins,
All	**pray for us.**
Leader	St. Michael,
All	**pray for us.**
Leader	St. Gabriel
All	**pray for us.**
Leader	St. Raphael,
All	**pray for us.**
Leader	All you Holy Angels and Archangels,
All	**pray for us.**
Leader	St. John the Baptist,
All	**pray for us.**
Leader	St. Joseph
All	**pray for us.**
Leader	All you Holy Patriarchs and Prophets
All	**pray for us.**

Leader invites members to name their favorite saints. After each name, all respond "pray for us."

Leader	All you holy men and women
All	**pray for us.**

Sharing Our Good News

The leader invites members of the group to share how they lived the Good News since their last meeting.

Reflection 1

Sacramentals

When I was a little girl my parents took my sisters and me to the Basilica of Our Lady of Guadalupe, and it was there that I received the sacrament of Confirmation. In Mexico most women are named "Maria" or "Guadalupe" to honor and ask for protection of Our Lady of Guadalupe. Those names may not appear on our birth certificate but you can be sure either name will be on our baptismal certificate.

I remember my mother setting up an altar with the image of Our Lady of Guadalupe and praying the rosary for nine days before her feast day which is December 12. For us it was one of the signs Christmas was coming. The celebrations of Our Lady of Guadalupe would lead us into the beautiful decorations and the *posadas* in preparation for the coming of Jesus.

On the feast day, around 5 a.m., my family would go to Church to sing the *mañanitas* to our Blessed Mother and to celebrate Mass. Afterwards we would have a real Mexican party with traditional dances while parishioners ate *tamales con champurrado* (hot milk with corn flour and chocolate). I especially enjoyed the *mariachis* during Mass and on the streets of my neighborhood. Friends and relatives of the women who are named Guadalupe are serenaded in celebration of such special day.

All Christian spirituality is founded in and nourished by the Paschal Mystery. Every baptized person is called to develop a personal spirituality so as to live it out in daily life. Sacramentals, which draw power from the Paschal Mystery, "prepare us to receive grace and dispose us to cooperate with it" (*CCC*, 1670). Spiritual devotions help us deepen our spirituality, become more open to God, and thus enable us to live the gospel values more fully.

Sacramentals include actions and objects such as crucifixes, holy water, rosaries, medals, scapulars, relics, incense, blessed palms, and the sign of the cross. The sacramentals are instituted by the Church "to sanctify certain ministries, states of life, and the variety of situations in which Christians are involved. Their use has been guided by bishops' pastoral decisions in responding to specific needs that are particular to a given period of history or locality. They include a prayer, usually with a gesture such as the Sign of the Cross or the sprinkling of holy water" (*USCCA*, p. 295). Sacramentals are means that the Church offers us as we strive toward our heavenly goal.

The sacramentals have foundations both in the Old and New Testaments. All the furnishings in the sanctuary were consecrated through anointing with holy oil (Exodus 40:9-11). The blessings given by the patriarchs to their children were considered very efficacious and irrevocable (Genesis 27:27). Jesus himself blessed the children "placing his hands on them" (Mark 10:16) and asked the apostles to bless the households of those who welcomed them (Luke 10:5; Matthew 10:12f). Acts of the Apostles makes explicit reference to the use of the sacramentals: "So extraordinary were the mighty deeds God accomplished at the hands of Paul that when face cloths or aprons that touched his skin were applied to the sick, their diseases left them and the evil spirits came out of them" (19:11-12).

There are two types of sacramentals. The first, and most important, are blessings. They may or may not be part of liturgical celebrations. By our baptism, in virtue of the common priesthood of believers, we are all empowered to call down God's blessing on one another, places, and things. In virtue of Holy Orders, bishops and priests are empowered to call down God's blessing in the celebration of the sacraments. Apart from sacramental ordination, other blessings for persons include the blessing of the abbot or abbess of a monastery, the consecration of virgins and widows, the rite of religious profession, and the blessing of certain ministries of the Church (readers, acolytes, catechists, etc.). Churches and altars may be dedicated and blessed, as may holy oils, vessels, and vestments.

Second, in addition to blessings, the church has also instituted sacred signs, pious objects, and religious ceremonies as sacramentals. The sign of the cross, the imposition of hands, the crucifix and statues, miraculous medals, icons, and relics of the saints are some examples of this type of sacramental.

Sacramentals are not sacraments in which grace is conferred by the power of the rite; with sacramentals grace is conferred through the faith and devotion of those who are using, receiving, or celebrating the sacramental. Sacramentals extend the liturgical life of the Church into our daily experience. These devotional objects, words, and actions are another means of sanctifying our daily lives and making them sacramental. The Church blesses and approves this practice because of her appreciation of what the Catechism calls "the Sacramental Economy" (see *CCC*, 1076). God's communication to us is not only through ideas and thoughts but also through created realities that remind us of God's presence and guidance. That's why the Second Vatican Council taught: "There is scarcely any proper use of material things which cannot thus be directed toward the sanctification of men and the praise of God" (*Sacrosanctum concilium*, 79).

If we examine our daily lives we may be surprised at just how often we invoke the blessings of God throughout the day. The sign of the cross that we often make reminds us of the presence of the Trinitarian God with us. Sprinkling with the holy water recalls to us our baptismal calling. Wearing a crucifix or placing it in a prominent place in our home or office reminds us of the Lord Jesus and the redemption he won for us. Thus sacramentals, understood and used correctly, can help us to live the challenge St. Paul gives us to "pray constantly" (1 Thessalonians 5:17; Ephesians 6:18).

Spotlight on the *Catechism*

"Among sacramentals, *blessings* (of persons, meals, objects, and places) come first. Every blessing praises God and prays for his gifts. In Christ, Christians are blessed by God the Father 'with every spiritual blessing' (Ephesians 1:3). This is why the Church imparts blessings by invoking the name of Jesus, usually while making the holy sign of the cross of Christ."

Catechism of the Catholic Church, 1671

Pondering the Word

'Blessed are they …'

Matthew 5:1-12

Take a few minutes to savor a word, a phrase, a question, or a feeling that rises up in you. Reflect on this quietly or share it aloud.

Sharing Question

• Through the Beatitudes, Jesus invokes God blessing on those in particular situations in life. How have you experienced God's blessing when in any of these states of life? What part do blessings play in your faith life?

Reflection 2

Devotions

Christians often join with members of their parish or diocesan community to visit shrines of Mary or the saints, visit the Holy Land, or Rome, the heart of the Catholic Church. In addition, we may regularly light candles in our churches, participate in novenas or belong to prayer groups that foster devotion. Many Catholics wear medals, honor relics of the saints, or carry rosary beads with them in their purse or pants pocket. We reverence icons, hang holy pictures, pray before statues of Jesus, the Holy Family, the angels or the saints.

All these actions and objects are personal forms of piety and devotion. They are a strong part of our identity as Catholics and recognized as a means to lead "the faithful to a deeper sense of their membership of the Church, increasing the fervor of their attachment and thus offering an effective response to the challenges of today's secularization" (Pope John Paul II, *The Church in America*, 16). The faithful practice of appropriate spiritual devotions nurtures our prayer life, deepens our relationship with God, and helps us to enter more actively and benefit more fully from the celebration of the sacraments.

Sacramentals and devotions support and complement our celebration of the sacraments. Unfortunately, misunderstanding on the part of some Catholics leads to a kind of superstitious practice or leads people of other religious persuasions to misinterpret Catholic use of sacramentals such as the rosary and statues. Personal use of sacramentals and practice of personal devotions are subject to "the care and judgment of the bishops and to the general norms of the Church" (CCC, 1676). The United States bishops explain that "popular devotions cannot be traced directly back to the ministry of Jesus and the practice of the Apostles. Most developed gradually over the years and even centuries as people sought ways of living out their faith" (*Popular Devotional Practices: Basic Questions and Answers*, 1). They go on to explain that devotions such as the rosary and scapulars have their roots in the practices of religious orders while others, such as devotion to the Sacred Heart or Miraculous Medal, originate from private revelation.

Devotions such as the practice of prayerful Scripture reading, Lectio Divina, and reading of spiritual books (e.g., lives of the saints) draw us more deeply into God's Word and teach us to listen and respond to his call in our daily lives. The traditional Catholic practice of praying the rosary brings us into a prayerful meditation on the mysteries of salvation and unites us with God. Novenas in honor of saints are opportunities for us to praise God who bestows his blessings upon us through the intercession of holy men and women. In recent years, the Divine Mercy devotion has become popular as it invites people to focus on the infinite mercy of our God who is all love and compassion.

Sharing Our Faith

• Which sacramentals have meaning in my faith life, and why?

• How do my devotional practices serve to nurture the prayer life of my parish or family?

Living the Good News

Determine a specific action (individual or group) that flows from your sharing. This should be your primary consideration for choosing an action.

If choosing an individual action, determine what you will do and share it with the group. If choosing a group action, determine who will take responsibility for different aspects of the action.

The following are secondary suggestions:

• Examine the sacramentals you have in your home. Reflect on their meaning and how they draw you to God.

• Participate in a novena or prayer group that prays the Rosary. Pay attention to the words and rhythm of your praying. Journal any thoughts or feelings that rise in you.

In light of this session, this week I commit to:

_____

_____

Lifting Our Hearts

Select a mystery of the rosary and pray a decade of the rosary together. Conclude by offering spontaneous prayers for loved ones.

Looking Ahead

• Prepare for your next session by prayerfully reading and studying:

  ▪ Session 12: Sacred Time & Sacred Space: Heaven on Earth;

  ▪ Scripture: 2 Corinthians 6:1-10;

  ▪ pages 170-177 from Chapter 14, "The Celebration of the Paschal Mystery of Christ," in the *United States Catholic Catechism for Adults*;

  ▪ paragraphs 1163-1199 of the *Catechism of the Catholic Church*;

• Remember to use RENEWING FAMILY FAITH and its helpful suggestions on how to extend the fruits of your sharing beyond your group, especially to your families (see pages 96-97).

Sacred Time & Sacred Space: Heaven on Earth

Suggested Environment

Bible, candle, and a small table on which a Bible may be enthroned. Consider decorating the table with colors of the liturgical year and a copy of Christian Prayer.

In addition it is suggested that the Catechism of the Catholic Church (CCC) *and the* United States Catholic Catechism for Adults (USCCA) *be available.*

Begin with a quiet, reflective atmosphere.

Lifting Our Hearts

Song Suggestion

"Eye Has Not Seen," Marty Haugen (GIA)

Prayer

For this antiphonal prayer, divide the group into two parts.

Leader	For everything there is a season and a time for every matter under heaven.
Side 1	A time to be born,
Side 2	and a time to die;
Side 1	a time to plant,
Side 2	and a time to pluck up what is planted;
Side 1	a time to kill,
Side 2	and a time to heal;
Side 1	a time to break down,
Side 2	and a time to build up;
Side 1	a time to weep,
Side 2	and a time to laugh;

Side 1	a time to mourn,
Side 2	and a time to dance;
Side 1	a time to throw away stones,
Side 2	and a time to gather stones together;
Side 1	a time to embrace,
Side 2	and a time to refrain from embracing;
Side 1	a time to seek,
Side 2	and a time to lose;
Side 1	a time to keep,
Side 2	and a time to throw away;
Side 1	a time to tear,
Side 2	and a time to sew;
Side 1	a time to keep silence,
Side 2	and a time to speak;
Side 1	a time to love,
Side 2	and a time to hate;
Side 1	a time for war,
Side 2	and a time for peace.

All

**God, Source of all life,
we pray that we may come
to accept and honor all those times,
both the joyful and the sad,
the easy and the unpleasant—
the light and the dark sides of life.**

**It is in this paradox
that we come to know you
and in knowing you,
we find the love
for which we are always searching.**

**Bring us to that love
through the sacramental graces
earned for us by your Son, Jesus Christ,
and through the power of your Holy Spirit.**

Amen.

(Based on Ecclesiastes 3:1-8, from The People's Prayer Book: Personal and Group Prayers, *published by RENEW International)*

Sharing Our Good News

The leader invites members of the group to share how they lived the Good News since their last meeting.

Reflection 1

Sacred Time

In the Disney Pixar movie *Up* we meet Carl Fredricksen, a widower, who is mourning the death of his wife, Ellie. In their younger days, the couple dreamed of traveling to Paradise Falls in South America where their childhood hero, renowned explorer Charles F. Muntz, had claimed to have discovered the skeleton of a giant bird. Unable to have children, the couple saved their money in hopes of traveling to Paradise Falls but always ended up spending it on other necessities. After Ellie passes away, Carl decides to fulfill their dream by traveling to Paradise Falls. Being a retired toy balloon vendor Carl attaches hundreds of thousands of balloons to the house he and his wife had lived in and begins his airborne journey to their dream destination.

After a wild ride he lands their house on the cliff of Paradise Falls. Carl sits in his worn, well-used armchair and opens up Ellie's scrapbook in which she had collected pictures and articles about the falls. Page after page, he recalls their many talks about visiting this special place. As he turns the pages of the scrapbook, he comes to pictures of their life together. Among the pictures, he finds a note from Ellie thanking him for "the adventure." Paradise Falls was a special place they had both dreamed of visiting, but at that moment Carl realized how much they each had treasured the time they had together.

When Jesus said that the Temple in Jerusalem would be destroyed, the disciples asked, "Tell us, when will this be, and what will be the sign that all these things are about to be accomplished?" (Mark 13:4). This question, as Jesus understood, had a double

Spotlight on the *Catechism*

"In its earthly state the Church needs places where the community can gather together. Our visible churches, holy places, are images of the holy city, the heavenly Jerusalem, toward which we are making our way on pilgrimage.

"It is in these churches that the Church celebrates public worship to the glory of the Holy Trinity, hears the word of God and sings his praise, lifts up her prayer, and offers the sacrifice of Christ sacramentally present in the midst of the assembly. These churches are also places of recollection and personal prayer."

Catechism of the Catholic Church, 1198-1199

meaning: First, "When will the temple be destroyed?" and, second, "When will everything it stands for come to an end?" These questions are based in two concepts of time, which would have been familiar to the Jews. There is a sort of cosmic time and there is a historical time. Cosmic time is cyclical; it does repeat and it is read by believers as a sign of the order stamped on creation by the Creator. History is about events and moments that are unique. The Old Testament brings these two concepts together in Exodus when God works within history to free his people. This event is celebrated in the present tense in the annual feast of Passover.

> "When the Church celebrates the mystery of Christ, there is a word that marks her prayer: 'Today!'—a word echoing the prayer her Lord taught her and the call of the Holy Spirit (cf. Matthew 6:11; Hebrews 3:7-4:11; Ps 95:7). This 'today' of the living God which man is called to enter is 'the hour' of Jesus' Passover, which reaches across and underlies all history."
>
> *Catechism of the Catholic Church,* 1165

The Greek terms for these two concepts of time were *chronos* and *kairos*. *Chronos* refers to the chronological measurement of time in years, months, weeks, days, hours, minutes, and seconds. We keep track of it with calendars, appointment books, and alarm clocks, etc. *Kairos* refers to the fullness of time when a particular event is to take place. How did the magi/wise men know that it was time for the King of Kings to be born? Not because they had a particular date on their calendar. They had seen the sign, the star in the East.

We humans who are bound by time (*chronos*) are invited, through the liturgy, to experience the fullness of time (*kairos*), the unfolding of God's plan of salvation through the Paschal Mystery of Jesus Christ. Christ's saving work is celebrated in every liturgy with particular aspects of the Paschal Mystery celebrated on certain days, weeks, and seasons of the year. The liturgical calendar as a whole is designed to unfold the whole Mystery of Christ, past, present, future: "Thus recalling the mysteries of the redemption, [the Church] opens up to the faithful the riches of her Lord's powers and merits, so that these are in some way made present in every age; the faithful lay hold of them and are filled with saving grace" (*CCC*, 1163, quoting *Sacrosanctum concilium*, 102).

These celebrations, as we saw in session two, are "signs of the new covenant;" a covenant that is "new and eternal." The liturgical year is not just the memorial of past events: It is making them present "now" as we live in hope for their complete fulfillment at the end of time. "Sunday, the 'Lord's Day,' is the principal day for the celebration of the Eucharist because it is the day of the Resurrection. It is the pre-eminent day of the liturgical assembly, the day of the Christian family, and the day of joy and rest from work. Sunday is 'the foundation and kernel of the whole liturgical year' (*Sacrosanctum concilium*, 106)" (*CCC*, 1193). By a tradition handed down from the Apostles, the Church celebrates the Easter mystery every Sunday, appropriately called the Lord's Day. It is the day of the Lord because it is the day "when the faithful gather 'to listen to the word of God and take part in the Eucharist, thus calling to mind the Passion, Resurrection, and glory of the Lord Jesus, and giving thanks to God …' (*Sacrosanctum concilium*, 106)" (*CCC*, 1167).

"In the liturgical year the various aspects of the one Paschal mystery unfold" (*CCC*, 1171). The liturgical year begins with Advent, which is four weeks of preparation for the birth of Jesus; it continues with Christmas to the feast of the Baptism of the Lord; Ordinary Time (weeks between the Baptism of the Lord and the beginning of Lent); Lent (forty days to prepare for Easter); Holy Week (beginning with Palm Sunday, a week commemorating the events leading up to and through the crucifixion of Jesus); Easter (fifty days celebrating the resurrection and Ascension of Christ); Pentecost (celebrates the manifestation of the Holy Spirit and birth of the Church); and Ordinary Time (weeks between Pentecost and Advent).

At the very center of the liturgical year is the feast of Easter. "Beginning with the Easter Triduum as its source of light, the new age of the Resurrection fills the whole liturgical year with its brilliance" (*CCC*, 1168). Easter is not just one feast among others. Easter is the foundation from which all other feasts come.

In addition, there are six holy days of obligation: Solemnity of Mary, Mother of God, Jan. 1; Ascension, forty days after Easter; Assumption of Mary, Aug. 15; All Saints' Day, Nov. 1; Immaculate Conception, Dec. 8; and Christmas, Dec. 25.

As part of the annual cycle, the Church honors holy men and women as models for us to emulate. Foremost among these is the Blessed Mary, Mother of God, whom "the Church admires and exalts the most excellent fruit of redemption and joyfully contemplates, as in a faultless image, that which she herself desires and hopes wholly to be" (*CCC*, 1172, quoting *Sacrosanctum Concilium*, 103). Martyrs and saints are honored through memorials.

The Liturgy of the Hours is a means through which we take the Paschal Mystery that we celebrate in the Sunday Eucharist into the rest of the week. This public prayer of the Church, also called "the divine office," is "so devised that the whole course of the day and night is made holy by the praise of God" (CCC, 1174, quoting *Sacrosanctum concilium*, 84; 1 Thessalonians 5:17; Ephesians 6:18). It is intended to become the prayer of the whole people of God; hence the laity too is encouraged to pray it.

Through the liturgical cycle, we recognize how God has sanctified time and we celebrate God's constant presence with us.

Now listen attentively as Paul offers a Christian perspective on time.

Pondering the Word

'Now is the acceptable time'

2 Corinthians 6:1-10

Take a few minutes to savor a word, a phrase, a question, or a feeling that rises up in you. Reflect on this quietly or share it aloud.

Sharing Question

• Recall a time when you felt you had experienced God's time (*kairos*). Share what it was like for you.

Reflection 2

Sacred Space

Because God created the Earth and said it was good we know that the whole Earth is sacred. Hence in one sense worship cannot be confined to any particular location. But from ancient times, people have built temples, shrines, and altars as designated places of God's presence. For the Jewish people, the Temple was a sacred place that assured the presence of God in the midst of the people. With the destruction of the Temple, and the exile of the Judeans to Babylon (587 BC), there could be no more morning and evening sacrifices. But the exiled people continued to gather as a community for prayers of praise and thanksgiving, adding several additional prayer times during the day. This structure of ongoing prayer served to strengthen the faith of not only the individual but the community during a time of isolation. Once the Jewish people returned from exile, there grew up the dual-channel practice of local synagogue prayer and restoration of the Temple worship.

After the earthly life of Jesus was over, the early followers of Jesus continued to use the synagogue for their Sabbath observance until they were barred for claiming that Jesus was the promised Messiah. Thus they began to gather in private homes. This practice continued for the first three centuries due to Roman persecution of Christians until freedom of religion was guaranteed by Emperor Constantine. From then, the underground church was able to use public places for worship.

In the Gospel of Matthew, the Greek word for church, *ekklesia*, is used to refer to the community of disciples (16:18, 18:17). *Ekklesia* later came to refer to the place where the Christian community gathered for worship. The *Catechism* teaches us that the church is "a house of prayer in which the Eucharist is celebrated and reserved, where the faithful assemble, and where is worshipped the presence of the Son of God our Savior, offered for us on the sacrificial altar for the help and consolation of the faithful—this house ought to be in good taste and a worthy place for prayer and sacred ceremonial" (10,5; cf. *Sacrosanctum concilium*, 122-127) (CCC, 1181, quoting *Presbyterorum ordinis* 5; cf. *Sacrosanctum concilium*, 122-127). It is for this reason that the Church gives specific guidelines for constructing church buildings in a beautiful and dignified way in order to reflect the sacredness of the people who gather there and of what they do there. Churches, with their art, architecture, and sacred images, should contribute to an environment of prayer.

The building is important, but the worshipping community is more important as the worshippers are the "living stones," gathered to be "built into a spiritual house" (1 Peter 2:5). The Second Vatican Council restored the New Testament vision of Church as "the people of God" (*Lumen gentium*, 15-16). Through Baptism, Christians become temples of the Holy Spirit, living stones out of which the Church is built.

Sacred space is not to be understood as limited to designated church buildings only. Every home where the family strives to be a domestic church is a sacred place. Every place becomes sacred when and where two or three are gathered in the name of Jesus.

Sharing Our Faith

• How do you make the times and spaces in your life sacred?

• The Second Vatican Council said that the word "church" refers to the building where we worship as well as the people gathered to worship. How do you experience "church" in your small Christian community?

Living the Good News

Determine a specific action (individual or group) that flows from your sharing. This should be your primary consideration for choosing an action.

If choosing an individual action, determine what you will do and share it with the group. If choosing a group action, determine who will take responsibility for different aspects of the action.

The following are secondary suggestions:

• Arrange to tour your church as a group. Then meet together to faith share on how the architecture, artwork, and sacred images contribute to a sense of sacredness.

• Obtain a liturgical calendar to use it to help you enter into the Paschal Mystery of Jesus Christ. Participate in Masses celebrated on holy days, feast days, and special observances. Pay special attention to the colors of the liturgical seasons as well as the color of the day as indicated by vestment insignia.

• Pray the Liturgy of the Hours in your faith-sharing group.

In light of this session, this week I commit to:

_____

_____

Lifting Our Hearts

Pray together

With tender compassion and transforming power
you come among us, O God,
making us members of your household,
"built upon the foundation of the apostles and prophets
with Christ Jesus himself as the cornerstone."

Strengthen us in faith:
expand our vision and fill us with the hope of your Spirit
that together we may build up your dwelling place,
ourselves becoming its "living stones."

Let the house which rises be a "living witness,
that all people may be lifted up
by the hope of a world made new."

We ask this through our Lord Jesus Christ, your son,
who lives and reigns with you
in the unity of the Holy Spirit,
God forever and ever.
Amen.

("Living Stones," by Fr. Edward Hislop, based on Ephesians 2:19b–20, 22; 1 Peter 2:5; Eucharistic Prayer for Various Needs and Occasions IV)

Looking Ahead

- Between Seasons of *Why Catholic?* continue meeting to faith share. Consider using the edition of PrayerTime: *Faith-Sharing Reflections on the Sunday Gospels* that matches the liturgical year year (see page 98 for more details).

- Remember to use Renewing Family Faith and its helpful suggestions on how to extend the fruits of your sharing beyond your group, especially to your families (see pages 96-97).

Why Catholic?
Resources from RENEW International

RENEWING FAMILY FAITH: Family faith-sharing bulletins

RENEWING FAMILY FAITH is a resource designed to extend the experience of the *Why Catholic?* process so that the faith sharing it promotes can become an integral part of whole family catechesis.

For every session offered by the *Why Catholic?* faith-sharing books there is a corresponding practical, informative two-page bulletin in full color: a total of 48 in all (12 for each of the four *Why Catholic?* faith-sharing books).

Each issue offers:
• an interesting selection of faith reflections for parents
• a wide variety of family activities
• questions that encourage table sharing
• brief Scripture passages and wisdom quotes
• an inspiring story on the life of an honored saint
• or a modern person who has lived an extraordinary faith life

This is a resource which can serve in a variety of creative ways: to reach and assist those whom for some reason are unable to take part in the Sunday celebration of Mass: those who are sick or homebound. It can also be used in sacramental preparation programs, and for homily preparation.

These Bulletins have been produced to facilitate sharing within the family on exactly the same themes the adults are exploring together in their *Why Catholic?* faith-sharing sessions.

God Acts in the Liturgy	Prodigal Father
Sacraments and Life	Anointing of the Sick
The Work of God	Mission of Service
Baptism Tradition	Love and Marriage
Confirming Faith	Laity in Community
In Jesus' Memory	Christian Initiation/Mission

Also available in Spanish.

A sample pack of the RENEWING FAMILY FAITH BULLETINS is included in the *Why Catholic?* Parish Kit. These Bulletins are fully presented in the *Why Catholic?* section of the RENEW International webstore: **www renewintl.org/store**

SONGS FOR FAITH SHARING
on the Celebration of the Christian Mystery

This CD offers recorded versions of all twelve songs that are suggested in this book for the moments of prayer during the faith-sharing sessions.

This song CD is available on **www renewintl.org/store**

GLEANINGS: A Personal Prayer Journal

"Journaling is an ancient, yet contemporary way to record our thoughts or feelings after we have prayed. … When we journal we come to new realizations about ourselves and our relationship with God, with other persons, and with all creation." —From the *Introduction*

Gleanings: A Personal Prayer Journal is a valuable tool for both avid and occasional journal writers. Each of the handsomely decorated pages offers a spiritual quotation or musing that can inspire the user to prayerfully reflect on his or her relationship with God.

The comfortably-sized format is conducive to many different methods of journaling: writing, poetry, or even sketching. The book is ring-bound, so pages lie flat, ready for your contribution. An excellent companion for your personal faith journey, *Gleanings* will help you tap into the richness of God's wisdom within you.

Gleanings is available on **www.renewintl.org/store**

Why Catholic? online

Visit our website at **www.renewintl.org** where you will find news updates about *Why Catholic?* and the other faith-sharing processes and resources that RENEW International offers.

PRAYER*TIME:*
Faith-Sharing Reflections on the Sunday Gospels

PRAYER*TIME* is a faith-sharing resource book, based on the Sunday Gospel reading. The themes for reflection have been designed so that they can be used either personally or in a group.

Each book offers gentle but insightful reflections that help the Gospel come alive. Written in an easy-to-read style that leads to profound questions about faith, each session sheds light on everyday life and should bear fruit in realistic action.

PRAYER*TIME* is published in three editions, one for each of the three years in the Sunday liturgical cycle.

This resource is also available in Spanish, again for each of the three years of the Sunday liturgical cycle, as O*REMOS: Reflexiones sobre los Evangelios Dominicales para Compartir la Fe.*

Longing for the Holy: Spirituality for Everyday Life
Based on selected insights of Ronald Rolheiser, O.M.I.

Ideal for faith-sharing or individual reflection, *Longing for the Holy* covers different dimensions of contemporary spiritual life, and allows participants to experience how the gentle spiritual guidance and practical wisdom of best-selling author, Fr. Ronald Rolheiser, O.M.I., can enliven everyday life.

The *Longing for the Holy* participant book includes 12 sessions and is ideal for all who want to enrich their sense of the presence of God and develop a deeper spiritual journey, whether as individuals or as a faith-sharing group. This resource addresses the way we channel the deep longing at the core of our beings and explores the implications of the central mysteries of the Catholic faith for spirituality: the Trinity, the Incarnation, the Eucharist, and the Paschal Mystery. Attending to the cultural challenges that keep us from realizing our true desire, it considers the important themes of Church community, justice, sexuality, the practices of the spiritual life, and being a mystic of the everyday.

The *Longing for the Holy* Kit is offered for those who are interested in following a group process. The Kit provides a wealth of resources, based on RENEW International's 30-year experience in promoting faith sharing.

A complementary resource is available in Spanish as *Sedientos de Dios: Una espiritualidad para la gente de hoy.*

The IMPACT Series

The **IMPACT** Series offers a wide range of formative materials to deepen understanding and to strengthen practice of our Catholic faith. It includes topics on prayer, family and work relations, spirituality, sacraments, life issues, and social issues.

RENEW International Contact Information

All of the resources presented on pages 96-99, together with many other faith-sharing materials, can be found on RENEW International's secure webstore: **www.renewintl.org/store**

For inquiries, contact us at
  RENEW International
  1232 George Street, Plainfield, NJ 07062-1717
  Telephone (inquiries only): 908-769-5400
  Toll free (for orders only): 1-888-433-3221
  E-mail: WhyCatholic@renewintl.org, Resources@renewintl.org

World RENEW

Our *World RENEW* e-newsletter covers interesting topics on today's spiritual life, with behind-the-scenes stories and updates on RENEW International's work with parishes and small communities across the United States and abroad.

Find out more about our latest resources and services, and read special features on how you can be an integral part of the RENEW International family. The e-newsletter is published in an attractive color format several times a year. Previous editions are available in the "free downloads" section of our webstore: **www.renewintl.org/store**

You can sign up for a free subscription using the prepaid reply card that follows page 100. Or you can do this on line at **www.renewintl.org**. Click on the "GET INVOLVED" menu, then on "Get our newsletter."

Alternatively, you can request this free subscription by email to development@renewintl.org

Or contact our Development Department at
  RENEW International
  1232 George Street
  Plainfield, NJ 07062-1717
  Telephone: 908-769-5400

Notes

Enrich your experience of

W⬡Y CATHOLIC?
JOURNEY THROUGH THE CATECHISM

with *GLEANINGS: A Personal Prayer Journal*

An excellent companion for your personal faith journey, *GLEANINGS* will help you explore the insights and prayer promptings emerging from your *Why Catholic?* experience.

Each double-page of this handsomely-decorated book offers a spiritual quotation or musing that can inspire you to prayerfully reflect on your relationship with God.

The comfortably-sized format is conducive to many different methods of journaling: writing, poetry, or even sketching.

Order from our secure online bookstore at
www.renewintl.org/store
or by phone at 1-888-433-3221.

Use promo code **WCGLE10** for a special *Why Catholic?* discount on this item

Did you know ...?

RENEW International is a not-for-profit Catholic ministry organizat[ion] that has touched the lives of 25 million people in the United States a[nd] 23 other countries.

From the inner city and rural areas to remote parts of the developing world, RENEW International's priority is to serve all parishes who desire to renew their fai[th] and build the Church, regardless of their economic situation.

Throughout RENEW's dynamic history, individuals have generously reached out to support our mission.

Please join us by making a donation to RENEW International at **www.renewintl.org/donate.**

Interested in learning more about RENEW?

World RENEW, our free e-newsletter, covers interesting topics on today's spiritual li[fe] with behind-the-scenes stories and special features on RENEW International's work with parishes and small communities around the world.

To read more and explore how you can be an integral part of the RENEW Internatio[nal] family, please return this card or visit **www.renewintl.org/subscribe**

❏ I would like to receive free *World RENEW* newsletters via email.

❏ I would like to receive a catalog and more information on other fine faith-sharing resources from RENEW International.

❏ I would like to receive information about ways to support RENEW's mission.

Title (Circle one)   Ms.   Mrs.   Mr.   Sr.   Br.   Fr.   Other, please specify: _____

Name _____

Address _____

_____

Phone _____

Email _____

Required for your email subscription. Your email will not be shared with other parties.

Tear-out reply postcard

WC2010